ALL THOSE GIRLS IN LOVE WITH HORSES

ROBERT VAVRA

WILLIAM MORROW AND COMPANY INC.
New York 1981

This book is dedicated to all those girls . . .

Library of Congress Catalog Card Number 81-82876
ISBN: 0-688-00649-3

Color reproductions by Cromoarte. Barcelona. Spain
First Edition
1 2 3 4 5 6 7 8 9 10

Printed in Italy by Gruppo Editoriale Fabbri S.p.A., Milano

Designed by the author

4

CONTENTS

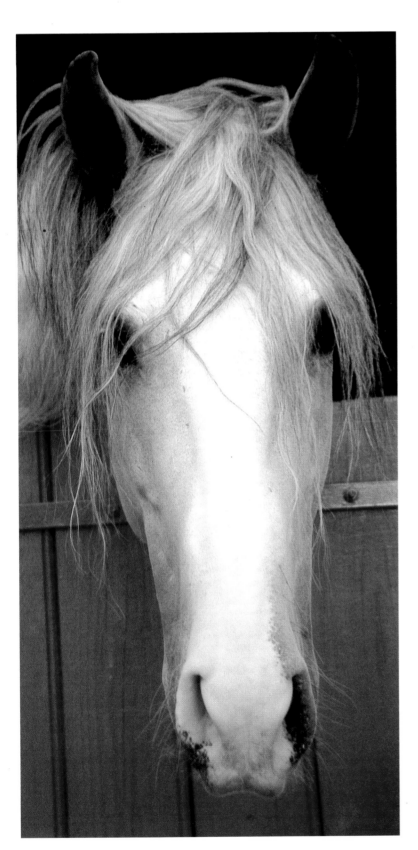

INTRODUCTION

"All those girls in love with horses! Researching my book on sport in America I ran into dozens of them," exclaimed James A. Michener, leaning back in the seat of the plane that was carrying us from San Diego to Denver. "They were working for practically nothing as grooms, or galloping horses. They weren't that interested in money, just in being close to the animals."

What Michener had said I also found to be true as over the next four years I moved about the world photographing and writing about equines. In all but Latin countries, the majority of people I knew who had outstanding careers with horses, or who loved them most, were women.

It is a fact that many girls, from childhood to adolescence, fix their attention on horses before they become interested in boys, who are dedicating their energies to competitive sports. What could be some of the reasons for this attachment? The horse is a romantic symbol with which the rider can identify; an uncontesting companion, a friend who does not impose conditions. Though huge and powerful, the horse can be shouted at, led around, punished and made to behave (most of the time). A parent reprimands his daughter, who then seeks out the horse for comfort ("Beauty,

love me no matter what I do") or sometimes behaves aggressively toward it in a display of dominance—the pecking order. The horse is a dependent creature that needs to be fed, watered, brushed and groomed; in general, mothered. It is a large, warm animal that can be sat upon, stretched out on, straddled, hugged, kissed and baby-talked to; an accepted object for physical affection, especially important perhaps in Anglo-Saxon societies where many people are inhibited about publicly touching, kissing and hugging. The horse means adventure; it is a vehicle to freedom, to joining and becoming one with nature.

Until recently when most schools did not offer sports, such as track and field, to females, the horse was the sportsminded girl's answer to that kind of fun and excitement. Using the horse, she could barrelrace, hunt, jump and engage in a dozen other competitive sports. However, the motive for this book is not to explore the reasons for a girl's attraction to horses, nor is it concerned with those early years in a girl's life when china horses fill her bookshelf, or when there may even be a real one in her backyard.

This book is about eleven outstanding young women who are leading rewarding lives centered on horses. Some of them are professionals, others are amateurs.

The word "girls" in the title is used as it is used by my eighty-year-old Aunt Bee when she speaks of playing cards with "the girls" (all of whom are over half a century old); it describes a state of mind. The ages of the women here range from sixteen to twenty-eight, though I have known some seventy-year-old girls who are just as dedicated to their careers, sports or animals as any of the women pictured in this book.

To take these photographs, I traveled from the February-frozen mountains of Canada to the August-baked plains of Spain, to Germany, England, France, Mexico, and to four states in the United States. And everywhere I visited I found that though my subjects spoke different languages, they demonstrated their dedication to and love for horses in much the same manner. All were highly professional in their approach to being the best in their fields.

As each young woman looks at the reader from these pages she also speaks out in her own voice—her own words—to tell about herself and her particular life with horses. From Canada Shannon Fleming's voice is heard, just as María Elena Castañeda tells her story from Mexico. Listen to what they have to say and watch while they demonstrate the joy and fulfillment that the love of horses has brought to their lives.

SHANNON FLEMING
canada

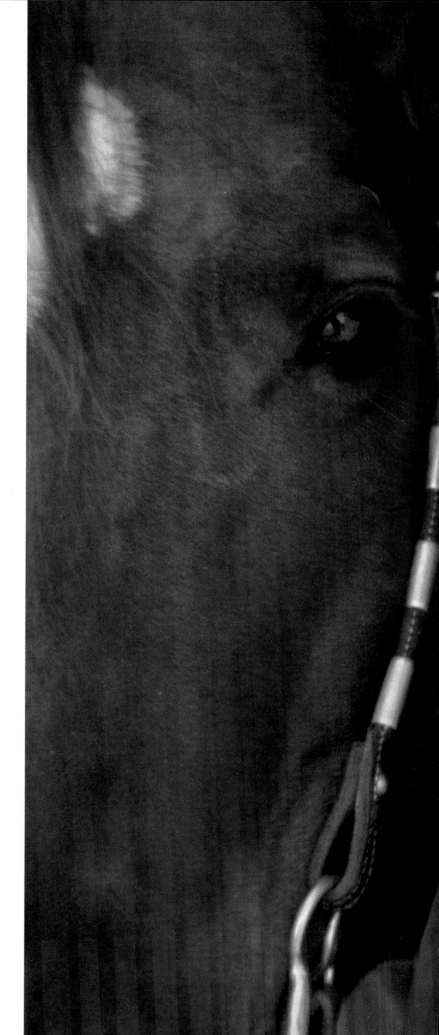

*W*hen the University of Calgary wrote to see if I would be their banquet speaker at a three-day symposium on horses, I took advantage of the opportunity to ask the Program Director to find an outstanding Canadian horsewoman for this book. Months later I was introduced to Shannon Fleming; good-looking, charming and well-educated Shannon is the only woman to win the Cutting Horse Championship of Canada—and she's done it twice.

It was February and there was snow on the ground when I arrived at Shannon's father's ranch to photograph her. Everyone had assumed that I would be working with Shannon in the indoor arena, so naturally there were puzzled faces when I explained I don't use artificial light and wanted to photograph cutting horses working in the snow. They said it would be dangerous to work cattle in the field, both for Shannon and for the horses, which were worth a great deal of money.

My disappointment must have showed, and after the problem was explained to Shannon, she agreed to try cutting cattle in the open field—but only as long as she felt her horse was not in danger.

Few examples of horse work have impressed me as much as the sight of Strato, Shannon's father's Quarterhorse stallion, in action. In most other equestrian activities I have photographed, the horse is clearly subordinate. Here, in the Canadian snowfields, I was watching a stallion on almost an equal basis with the cow. The reins in most of these photographs are completely slack, and the horse, while taking leg commands, is most often calling the shots himself. It was like seeing the horse on his own in the wild, not completely dulled and dominated by man, as Strato concentrated intently on each cow, anticipating its attempts to flee, rushing forward, lunging, feinting and stopping to block her escape and make impossible her return to the herd. How wonderful for the horse, I thought, to be able to utilize that natural herding instinct, that drive to dominate, that is such a primeval part of his nature.

On June 24, 1956, I was born in Edmonton, a city in central Alberta. My family moved to Calgary when I was still very young, and I have lived in and around Calgary for most of my life. I guess animals have always had a very special place in my life, for one of the first decisions I ever remember making was that stuffed animals took priority over dolls and games. Even my imaginary friend, whose name was Pawny, looked very much like a centaur, except that he could choose which part of him would be man and which part horse. I believe that the strength with which things of this world affect us has something to do with how much we need to learn what they have to teach us. The world often seems to be much like a gigantic school where we come to learn. Perhaps Pawny was a little symbolic of the way I chose to learn, for people and horses have always exerted the strongest effect on my life. Perhaps symbolic also is the way Pawny could switch parts of himself around—for although people were often to teach me about horses, horses were also to teach me about people.

One of the most influential people in my life, and the first person ever to teach me about horses, was my mother's father, my grandpa Nett. I called him Snooky, which must have been a term of strong endearment for me because even yet, as I think of him, his kind and gentle manner makes me warm and full inside. He always smoked a pipe and carried a cane, and he expressed his joy of life with every part of his being. Snooky was a cattle buyer, and I remember going out to the fields with him whenever our family was visiting. He had a special horn in his car that always fascinated me; when he sounded it the cattle would come walking over to where he had parked. Once in a while he would be buying horses as well, and I

(1) Twice Canadian Cutting Horse Champion Shannon Fleming with her Quarter-horse stallion, Strato Chief.
(3) Made of rawhide and horsehair, this hackamore (bosal) will be used on a young horse until he is completely broken to rein and is ready for the bridle and snaffle (4) or a grazing bit used for cutting (5).

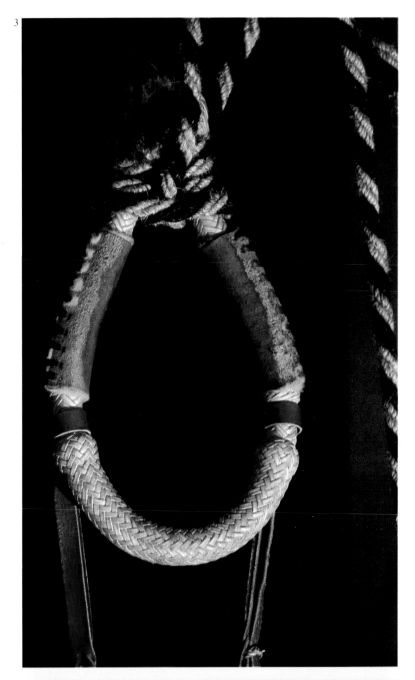

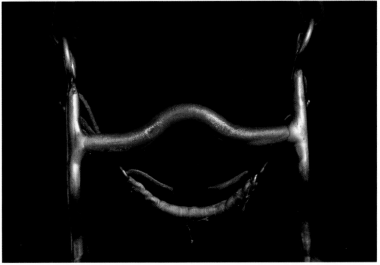

can still remember the way he used to inspect them. He would check their teeth and legs, and then he'd spend a long time looking at their eyes and watching the movement of their heads. Grandpa said that a horse's eye was the best mark of its worth. If its eyes were kind and soft, its honesty would always compensate for whatever it might lack in physical makeup.

When I was eight my family bought land outside Calgary, and my parents, who had always been sensitive to the whims and desires of their children, bought my sister Marilyn and me a horse. Smokey was rather a bad first experience, and after he had thrown all the family at least once, a decision was made to change horses. We let Snooky pick out the next horse. Grandpa found us two Welsh-Quarter-horse crosses, imaginatively named Blackie and Queenie. Blackie, all black with one white star on her head, was to be my horse for the next four years. When Marilyn and I wanted to start showing our horses, my parents arranged for us to take riding lessons.

Showing horses seems to act as a catalyst in a common chain of events that begins with exposure and eventually leads to increased acquisition of horseflesh. It wasn't long before Blackie was bred, and our family started making regular appearances at Quarter-horse sales. Dad seemed to be spending less time on the golf course and more time hauling horses and eating greasy hamburgers at the Quarter-horse shows and girls' rodeos. Mom was rapidly increasing the number of weekends spent sitting in wooden stands, as well as the number of evenings spent waiting for riding lessons to end. They never seemed to mind, though, and I wonder if they knew then that they would repeat this whole process with my brother, Bob.

It was during one of our weekly riding lessons that my instructor introduced me to a big sorrel gelding and a little

Here Shannon lunges (6) and then drives (7) Kilebar San, a four-year-old gelding in training who was foaled on the ranch and is a son of the Cutting Horse World Champion, Peppy San.

7

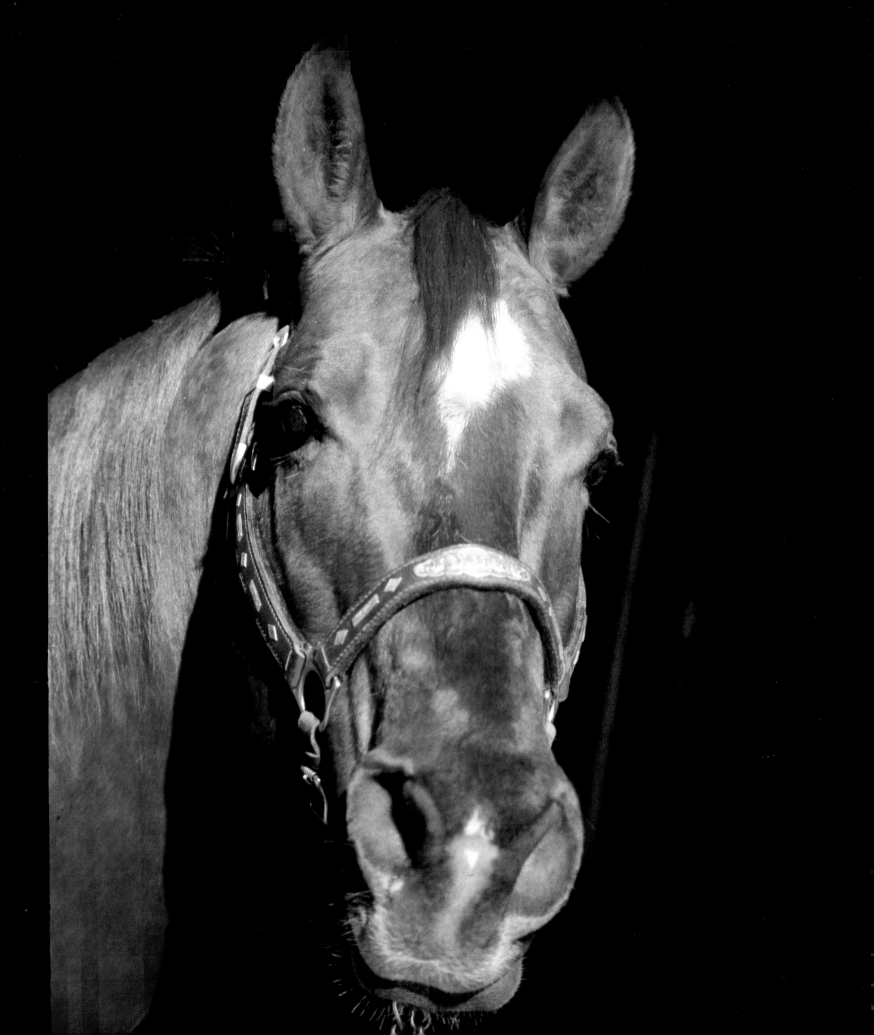

brown cow. I was thirteen at the time and had previously been showing Quarter-horses, barrel racing, goat tying and cow riding. My first encounter with a cutting horse, however, was not like anything I had ever experienced before, and although I continued these other events, they became rather secondary. By the time I was sixteen, all I really wanted to do was cut cattle. There was something about the horse's mind that was expressed more clearly through cutting than through any other sport involving horses that I had ever witnessed. The horse wasn't just reacting to the cow's movements, he was actually anticipating them. There was a higher level of perception involved in this skill, a quality I hadn't previously considered in horses, and the whole idea of it intrigued me.

At this time my dad owned a palomino mare named Sandy Gold that had originally been trained as a cutting horse. Sandy was fairly old and very solid, and she helped me to obtain a basic understanding of the sport. I tried to apply my limited knowledge to the young Quarter-horse gelding that I was showing at the time, but I had barely developed the ability to ride a trained cutting horse and, consequently, we spent most of our time going in and out of the herd.

It was during this time, too, that my grandpa Nett died. Mom put the money that grandpa left her into bank accounts for her three children. I put all the money from my account toward a little brown mare that had the kind and honest attitude grandpa had always valued; her name was Sassy Britches. Sassy was never very flashy or fancy, but her consistency always seemed to add up at the end of the season. We won the Canadian Girls' Rodeo Association cutting from 1971 until 1974, and I quickly grew to respect the value of her honest efforts. During this time Dad finally bought himself a cutting horse. Soon after, he built a barn and indoor arena so that we could work our horses on cattle all year long. In 1974 Sassy's legs began to stiffen up after she cut, and although it really wasn't noticeable when she was cutting, it didn't seem fair to ask any more of her. Although he never said anything about getting a new horse, I noticed that my father was beginning to make quiet inquiries when we went to the cuttings together.

Horses are very similar to people and individual animals can affect us very differently. Like people, some seem to be merely acquaintances who pass in and out of our lives with frequent regularity, others touch us a little deeper and through the sharing of present lives and common interests, we learn something of ourselves while growing through the experience. But every once in a while something or someone comes into your life and you know what it is to be fully alive, to be filled with whatever

9

(8) Strato Chief, a seven-year-old son of Peppy San, was born in Texas and came to Canada in 1977. (9) Shannon with stable pets Max, the St. Bernard, and Cat, the cat.

it is that life means to you. It's an experience that sets you apart from everyone else in the whole world and, at the same time, it gives you a feeling of belonging to the world and everything in it.

When Diane Kilebar first came into my life, I suppose I really didn't realize that she would provide this kind of experience for me, or even that she would have such a strong effect on my life. The times that I rode and competed on Diane never seem to exist merely as a memory, but have a very real relationship to the present. I guess that the meaning we attach to our experiences has a lot to do with the way we are approaching life when they occur. From the first time I saw Diane until the last time I rode her, I had been going to school and then to the university.

Life was a toss-up between coming to some understanding of myself and my world and having as much fun as possible. I tried to understand Diane as well; I tried to work out how she thought, I tried to get a feel for how she moved, but mostly I just tried to enjoy her as much as I could.

My earliest recollections of Diane are filed away in the same category as John Wayne and my grandpa Nett. They are the kind of memories that create an inspirational overflow whenever you pull them out. I was about fifteen and had been cutting for a couple of years. Dad had brought us to watch the open cutting at the Calgary Stampede, and I had that awed feeling like when our junior high volleyball coach took our team to watch a university game. My eyes skimmed back and forth across an arena of shiny, well-muscled horseflesh until all I saw was Diane. She was a deep golden color with a silvery-gray mane and tail. She had huge brown eyes that gazed into the distance like there was something really important out there. She wasn't very tall, but when all the horses lined up, she had the broadest chest and longest body in the arena. Diane didn't look stocky, though; her neck was long and slender and she had a refined look about her—a sort of powerful grace. The only reason I saw any other horses in the arena that day was to compare them to Diane—but they didn't. In fact, nothing in the whole world compared to Diane at that moment.

Diane was younger than most of the horses in the arena, yet none even came close to touching the style she had already developed. She would float across the arena, and when the cow turned, Diane's powerful hind end slid into the ground while her long neck and body changed direction in midair. She had an extended and graceful sweeping motion with her front legs and at times it almost appeared as if her entire body were completely horizontal. Her long mane and tail streamed in the

(10 & 11) Shannon leaves the stable to look for cattle. Today cutting is a carefully organized and highly specialized sport with rules to cover every aspect of showing and judging the cutting horse.

wind of her own speed, and her face seemed to radiate intelligence and sensitivity. Diane's ears moved continuously back and forth, expressing deep concentration, as she anticipated each new movement the cow would make. When the buzzer rang, she stopped and walked calmly back to the lineup, taking her place among the other horses. I looked into the distance to see what it was that she kept gazing at, but there was just the blue sky with the sun in it. I wondered what it was she saw out there.

I didn't see Diane at any of the cuttings after that, and my father said someone had bought her but wasn't going to show her. Two years passed and I had entered Sassy in a few of the open cuttings. We placed in a go-around here and there, but the open competitions were really tough for Sassy and the stiffness in her legs seemed to become a little more noticeable every time she had worked cows. One morning my parents called me down to the breakfast table and their eyes were twinkling so hard that I thought I'd forgotten my own birthday. Dad explained that he had bought himself a new horse, but that he didn't really have the time to ride her. He went on to say that I could ride and show her for a year, and that her name was Diane Kilebar.

When Diane first backed out of the trailer at our ranch, she wasn't quite as I had remembered her. Her coat wasn't nearly as shiny as it had been at the Stampede, her mane and tail were jagged and tangled, and the muscles that had once been full and firm were now soft and loose. Her big brown eyes seemed to have a quiet reserve about them, but I noticed her concentrated, intelligent gaze as she looked around, ears twitching and nostrils quivering, as if searching for some meaning to attach to her new environment. At first, we just loped around the arena and trotted out in the snow, getting used to one another. After several weeks Diane's muscles began to firm up, her wind increased until her breathing became steady and easy, and her coat was coming back to life.

I grew fond of Diane's gentle manner, for she never seemed to get excited or nervous, yet she was sharp and quick. When we were out in the snow, she would flare her nostrils, stick her neck way out and constantly look in all directions with an intense expression in her eyes. The way she would look around like that intrigued me, for although it made her seem aloof and distant, I was extremely curious about what was going on inside her. Other horses seemed content to eat, play and be ridden—but Diane acted as if there was something more for her.

The first time I remember feeling sure about what Diane was thinking was the first time I cut cattle with her. There was absolutely no doubt in my mind where her

(12) *Even though cutting has now been developed as a sport, cutting horses, trained to separate a cow from a herd and control it, are still essential in the field.*

concentration was directed. As the cattle moved into the arena, I noticed a slight trembling of horseflesh beneath me. Diane's ears shot straight forward, then twitched back and forth while her nostrils flared and her breathing became rather uneasy. As we entered the herd of cattle, now settled at the far end of the pen, her slender neck lowered and her steps became slow and cautious. I signaled my choice to Diane and she extended her nose, as if to intimidate the cow into moving from the herd. Once clear of the other cattle, the animal began to move into the sudden realization that it had been separated from the security of the herd. Diane's back legs suddenly folded into the ground while her whole front end descended. It felt like the arena floor had just dropped from beneath us, for her shoulders and neck were now level with the cow's. From a full run, Diane could slide her back legs deep into the ground while her front end snapped around so that, for an instant, it felt as if two parts of her faced opposite directions. She was so quick that at times I wasn't sure which direction I was facing myself, but her fluid and flexible movements made her feel smooth and easy. When a cow circled around in front of us, she would bury her hind end and extend her neck and legs in a side-to-side sweeping motion that seemed to cover half the width of the arena. Movements and sensations that I never knew existed were bursting into experience, and throughout the whole thing I had to keep reminding myself to breathe.

I rode and cut on Diane for the rest of that winter, and although things felt a bit off sometimes when we were working cows, I didn't feel any need for alarm. I just attributed our losing a cow here and there to the fact that we needed more time to get used to each other. As winter passed and the show season approached, I acquired increasingly stronger visions of Diane and me never losing a cutting. I'm not sure where the visions went, but I am very

Shannon follows a stray cow (13) and then brings it back to the herd (14). In a cutting contest a rider is given two and a half minutes to show his horse. The horse demonstrates, and is marked on, his ability to outthink the cow he is working (his cow sense) and to outmaneuver it.

15

clear where our entry fees were going, because for a while it seemed that losing was about all we could do. I couldn't figure out what was happening, because Diane was working her heart out, but we were always behind our cattle. My immediate reaction was to push her harder. This didn't help, but I couldn't think of a reasonable alternative and I just kept on pushing. I knew things were really getting bad when Diane started ringing her tail and pinning her ears in the herd, as if she didn't even want to be there. It sounds illogical, but the faster we went, the harder it became to catch a cow.

I had passed frustration and insecurity and was sinking into depression when I finally realized it might be useful to seek assistance from someone else. I remembered Fred

Duke, the man who had been riding Diane at the Calgary Stampede, and I called him up. Fred said he thought he could help me. I loaded up Diane and spent the next three hours on the highway, dissolving newly emerging visions. Visions, I had decided, were bad luck.

It turned out that visions weren't bad luck at all; in fact, it was my riding that had been bad luck. When Fred first explained that I was pushing Diane too hard, I wondered how this could be true if we were always behind our cattle. It took a while for me to catch on, but I finally realized

In a competition a horse is awarded points for his ability to enter quietly a group of cattle, and without unnecessary disturbance, to separate and drive a chosen animal from the herd. (15 & 16) Shannon and Strato prevent a cow from rejoining a herd in the open field.

that Fred was right. I was pushing too hard. In fact, I would push Diane twenty feet past the cow so that when the cow turned to go the other way, we'd be sitting twenty feet behind it. Realizing my position, I would panic and push even harder, which sent Diane even farther past the cow—and so began the vicious circle of push and chase. Somewhere along the line I had forgotten that when the cow stops, we should stop too.

Fred taught me how to watch the cow's head and try to rate its speed and direction so that I wouldn't be pushing when I should just be sitting. More important, he taught me to respect and trust Diane's ability and sensitivity. My constant interference and desire to control her movements were confusing us both, and he helped me to understand when she needed some gentle guidance. Fred

(17) The cow looks to its right, ready to flee in that direction to join the herd. (18) The cow starts its escape, but (19) is anticipated and halted by Strato. Before the animal can join the herd by running to its left (20), it is checked by Strato (21 & 22).

said that Diane knew she'd be in trouble if she ran that far past her cattle, but her sensitivity to my constant pushing caused her to do it anyway. Pinning her ears and ringing her tail were signs of justified frustration at being asked to do what she knew was wrong. Diane could read cattle better than I could ever hope to, and I quickly realized that if we were going to be a winning team, I was going to have to let her lead for a good part of the game.

I felt the results of Fred's guidance immediately, and after we left his place there became less and less need for visions. Why dream it when you can live it? We began to place often, and even win with increasing regularity. I was beginning to develop a valuable and necessary trust in Diane, for the more I learned not to interfere with her natural way of working, the better we seemed to do. I was never completely relieved of my need to control part of the action though, and we were to return to Fred many times over the next few years.

It seemed as if the rationale behind our cutting strategy carried over into our relationship. Before Diane, I had always felt that I knew more than the horse and therefore was the one to teach and care for it. Diane was different; I sensed an equality between us and, at times, even felt as if she could perceive things that were beyond my scope or understanding. My efforts to control her affections were about as futile as my efforts to control her cutting. Once in a while she would come to me, nuzzling for attention, or respond to me when I initiated the petting and scratching. I noticed, however, that when I tried to gain her recognition to assure myself that she needed me, or to show friends what a good relationship we had, Diane became very uninterested.

During that year together, cutting took on a new dimension for me; it was as if understanding Diane had somehow added meaning to what we did together. I had always loved the way she felt; her smooth flexibility and supple strength combined to create the sensation of riding a fast cloud. I found, however, that I gradually directed more and more of my attention to her thoughts rather than to her movements. My ability to pick up on her messages was increasing, for I began to sense when I pushed Diane too hard or rushed her too much, and the more I adapted to her natural style, the better we seemed to do. Diane and I won the Canadian Open Championship that year, and the excitement of my wildest dreams coming true was rather dampened by the fact that my year with her was up. During the awards banquet, my parents presented me with a gift that was to surpass any award ever created. They gave me the horse that I had grown to love and respect; they said that Diane was mine to ride and show forever.

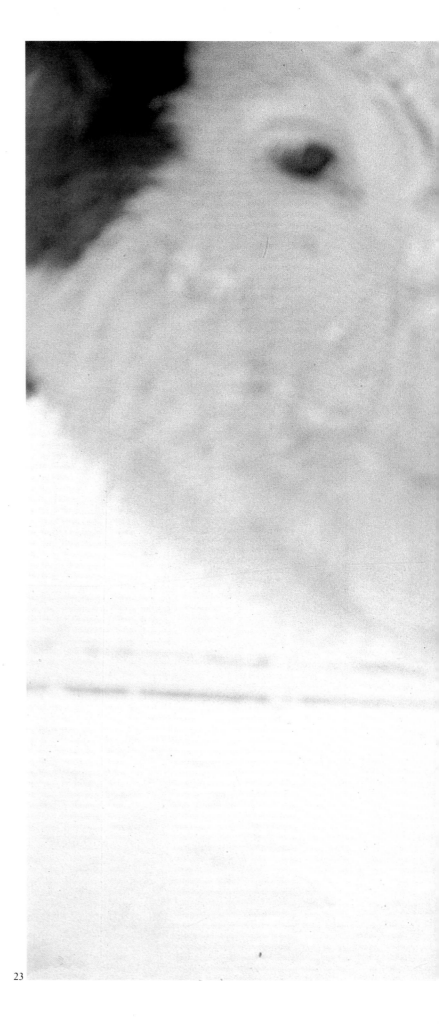

In (23) Strato holds the cow; the loose reins demonstrate the extent of the horse's independence from the rider. It is at this time that the intelligence and speed of the horse are shown most clearly.

23

I really believe that over the next few years Diane and I adapted to one another. I learned to leave her alone as much as I could, and when I got carried away with interference, she learned to ignore me as much as she could. It was as if she could split her mind, and while half of her would decide which of my instructions to ignore, the other half would concentrate on the cow. I must have been quite a challenge for her at times, and I'm sure that we often won in spite of my efforts. I didn't care though, for the sheer pleasure of riding her by far outweighed the pride I buried to give Diane the credit for winning. And

Shannon poses with a portrait of Diane (24). Some of the trophies that she has received in cutting-horse competitions (25 & 26). A silver buckle (27) is awarded to the Canadian Cutting Horse Champion.

every once in a while I felt as though something clicked between us and I didn't have any need to push or direct her at all. Things just seemed to unfold with this sense that everything would be all right—and it was, for it was during these times that we turned in our highest scores. I didn't concentrate on the cows, the turnback men, the time, or anything for that matter; I just became a part of what Diane was doing. Although these times were rare and infrequent, when they did happen I felt terrific, and when they were over I sensed a strong tie with Diane.

Diane's efforts carried us through two Canadian Open titles in 1975 and 1976, and won us the Canadian High Point title in 1978; and if winning then had still been a priority for me, I would have postponed her retirement well past 1978, for I realized that the likelihood of my ever riding another horse with Diane's abilities was remote. But that year, our last year at the Kamloops Rodeo, I began to feel that she was ready for motherhood. When the decision was made, I was teaching school, and by the time she was in foal for the second time, I had returned to the university to do postgraduate work in psychology. I'm still not sure that this is what Diane wanted, and wonder if the decision to retire her reflected more the changes in my own life than something I had picked up from her. I am sure, however, that the way my view of Diane has altered over the years reflects the direction my life has taken. As part of me searches for deeper meaning in human behavior, another part of me finds new meaning in Diane.

I found I had trouble adjusting to other horses after her and, although the next horse that I rode had tremendous ability, I knew that something was missing—it was hard for both of us to trust each other. Diane and I seemed to have reached a comfortable level of silent agreement. But my attitude to this task has altered because of knowing Diane.

26

KENDEL EDMUNDS

usa

Years ago when I was deeply involved in a behavioral study of the Spanish fighting bull, I often took books into the field to read during the hot midday hours in Andalusia, when the temperature was frequently 120 degrees, the bulls almost completely inactive and the light unsuitable for the kind of photographs I wanted. One of the books I remember best was Mary Renault's The King Must Die, which chronicled the adventures of Theseus; of most interest to me were her descriptions of bull dancing or vaulting. Being in the field with bulls, my imagination played with those images of man and beast performing together in ancient Crete.

Later, in Seville, I saw a comic bullfight spectacle in which one of the acrobats did some flat and scissor-leaps over a young bull and, even in that farcical setting, it caused me to sit on the edge of my seat. After that, whenever the comic troupe came to town, I went to the ring and sat through the show just to see those few seconds of bull-leaping.

When I first heard about horse vaulting, I was anxious and curious to see someone practicing it—it, too, seemed like one of those remnants of ancient Crete that had somehow survived in a more or less recognizable form.

It was Elizabeth Searle, president of the American Vaulting Association, who invited me to her dressage school in San Juan Bautista, California, where she and her partner, Jeff Moore, generously offered their home, time and help to make possible the photographs that are featured here.

As well as Kendel Edmunds, the International Vaulting Champion, I also photographed Sidney Stang, the Women's National Champion, Men's International Champion Brian Post, National Champion Kim Gussenhoven and Danny Baker. Watching those young people in action, I was conscious of the fact that until a few years ago vaulting was practically unknown in America, though it has long been a popular sport in Germany. Even more impressive is the fact that at the first International Vaulting Competition several years ago in Germany, it was the American team, working on an unfamiliar horse, that won the highest honors.

Horses, horses, horses, that's all I've ever thought about since I was little. When I first started wanting a horse of my own we lived in a place where horses were not allowed—I was born and raised in the San Francisco Bay Area. Soon after, however, we moved to Walnut Creek, where all our neighbors had horses. My mother had me start taking lessons from a friend so that when I got my own horse I would know how to ride.

My first experience with vaulting was not the most pleasant. I was up at horse camp and they were offering a vaulting class. Well, I had no idea what vaulting was, but I signed up anyway. The first day of vaulting came and I

was late! I finally found out where they were having the lesson, and once I was there the coach, Inez Fort, asked me who I was. I told her. She then accused me of not signing up. I told her I had, but she did not believe me. I did not exactly start out on the good side of Mrs Fort.

Mrs Fort explained to us that vaulting originated in Germany and was used to help troopers in the cavalry feel more at home on a horse. Other countries started to use vaulting the same way, and soon it evolved into a sport.

(1) International Vaulting Champion seventeen-year-old Kendel Edmunds with Pink Champagne.

Now in Germany the government subsidizes vaulting for children under sixteen years old. After you are sixteen you can no longer vault for free. Here in the United States you can be as old as you like, there is no age limit. There is no doubt though that vaulting is a sport for the young. It is very demanding physically, you have to be in good shape to vault seriously.

I would recommend it to anyone who likes an active sport. You do not have to be able to ride or do gymnastics, but it helps. The only thing to remember when you are learning to vault is to move with the horse, because rhythm is the most important thing. The problem most people have when they are learning is keeping up with the horse when they go to mount. Vaulting, like any sport, takes a little getting used to, but it sure is fun once you get the hang of it.

That first day we worked on the compulsories on the barrel. In vaulting there are six basic compulsories: Riding or Basic Seat, Flag, Mill, Flank, Stand and Scissors. The barrel is used for beginners so they do not waste the horse's energy; it also helps you get the feel of new moves without using the horse. After we had the compulsories down pretty well on the barrel, we moved on to the horse. It was easier for me than I expected; most of the compulsories were simple to do, except for Stand.

I vaulted the rest of the time I was up at camp. After horse camp was over, I did not really think about vaulting much until one day I decided I wanted to get back into it. I asked my mother to call Mrs. Fort and find out when the next lesson was. Once I started vaulting again, I began to improve.

There are three kinds of recognized competitions in vaulting: Regular Team competition, Three-Phase competition and International Individual competition. Regular Team competition requires each vaulter on the team (consisting of eight vaulters) to perform all six compulsories. All eight vaulters do Basic Seat, then Flag and so on till all the compulsories are finished. Then there is the Kür, or freestyle section, which is a routine consisting of singles, doubles and triples. Each vaulter must be in at least one Kür and the compulsories.

Three-Phase competition consists of ground and barrel routines and the compulsories on the horse. The ground routine is a three-minute freestyle performance to music. The barrel is a five-minute routine also to music. The compulsories are the same as for Regular Team competition, except that either the first or last three, or all six, are performed to the right. This depends on what level you are competing at.

The International Individual class has three segments: The first is the compulsories, performed continuously without a dismount between each one. The second is the first Kür routine; there are certain requirements that must be met and performed in the routine—maximum time, one minute. The third is the second Kür routine,

which has no requirements and may consist of anything the vaulter wants—maximum time, one minute.

Vaulting is scored on a 1-10 point system. A 10 is excellent; 9, very good; 8, good; 7, fairly good; 6, satisfactory; 5, sufficient; 4, insufficient; 3, fairly bad; 2, bad; 1, very bad; and 0, not performed. There are many things that may cost you points: for example, not holding an exercise long enough or being off count in your Mill. In freestyle routines you are awarded points for performance, degree of difficulty and general impression (how you presented yourself). When a team is scored, each vaulter receives points, but later they are all averaged together for the final score.

My first Fest (the biggest competition of the year) was in 1976. I was on the team (Fort's Flyers) and also in an individual class. The team competition went fine. We competed in C team (compulsories and Kür) and also in team Three-Phase, and placed well in both. I was so nervous before my individual class I could barely function. When I went to get on the horse, since I was so nervous, I did a basic mount rather than something original. The whole time during my routine (which was unbelievable, because it was so simple) all I thought was "straight legs and pointed toes." It came as quite a shock to me when I won the class and high point for my division. Looking back at that routine, I would say that the judges were more interested in form than difficulty, because now the quality of vaulting has increased so much. For a person to win a class now, the content of the routine must be as good as the performance.

Six months after the Fest, the American Vaulting Association announced they were sending a team over to Europe in the Summer of 1977. To try out for the team you had to be a silver medalist. No one on our team had

(2) Kendel and Pink Champagne on their way to the practice ring. (3) Instructress Joyce Post (left) and Inez Fort with Kendel and Inez's daughter, Ariana, examine a vaulting surcingle.

(mostly Stand) and two Kür routines. I did all right, but I could have done better. I fell off on almost everything I tried. I made it through about half of both my routines. We were using different horses and it was hard for me to adjust. After the first tryouts they had call-backs. I was one of the twenty-five who were called back. The judges had said I had not done so well at the first tryouts, but they felt I had potential. At the second tryouts Jeff put any two people together to perform doubles on the barrel and on the horse. We also had to do some more compulsories. We did not find out if we had made it or not for about a month after the second tryouts. Finally, Inez received a letter saying I had been chosen for the team. I was so excited when I heard, it really made that day special.

The summer before we went to Europe, we spent a month at training camp and we worked on everything. We worked on our compulsories constantly, on several different horses (many teams were nice enough to let us use their horses for a short time), because we had no idea what kind of horse we would use in Europe. We also worked on Kür; we all had to practice each other's parts as well as our own in case somebody got injured.

We left for Germany early in August. Once there, we vaulted twice a day, for two or three hours in the morning and evening. The horse we were given was a C-team horse that had never had triples done on him, and that's what our Kür mostly was. Jeff spent many sessions just working on the horse. After a while the horse would at least let us do triples on him, but he was not too happy with the situation. Our team Kür must have been rewritten at least once a day. The way it was written in the beginning was unfair because one person got to do all the good basing; it went from there and every day there would be a new Kür which was thought to be fair. This went on until Jeff wrote a Kür and said, "This is it, take it or leave it."

The big day we had all been working so hard for finally arrived. There were seven other teams competing in the B division, one from Holland, another from Switzerland and

ever taken a medal test. Our team decided to hold medal exams. Everyone passed except me. Inez really wanted me to try out for the team going to Europe, so two days before the trials Jeff Moore gave me a medal test. I flunked again. Inez was very embarrassed because she knew I could do it, but I kept making little mistakes. Also, I was not a very strong vaulter. Jeff said he would give me one more chance. I finally passed with a very low score of 63 percent. The reason I had such a difficult time passing the exam was because I was not really ready for it. Most vaulters go for their bronze medal before their silver, and they pass with a low score. I was also a rather unsteady vaulter at that time; I had not had a lot of work on the horse and had only been vaulting for eight months.

The day of the trials finally arrived. I was excited and nervous. That day we had to do some of the compulsories

the rest from Germany. They were all good. It was our turn to go into the ring; the whole team seemed a little edgy. We entered the ring, bowed to the judges and started our compulsories. It was deathly quiet in the ring; everyone was watching the Americans very intently. In Europe they perform their compulsories and Kür straight through; in America we rest between the two. It was a little difficult for us to get used to going straight through, but we managed. After the judges signaled they were ready, we began our Kür. The whole effect was very successful. There was only one small problem. The girl who was supposed to do the last dismount (which was a round off) was not able to get to her feet because the horse was so

Joyce Post and Kendel braid a horse's mane (4) and tail (5) before an exhibition. (6) Kendel has her own hair plaited. (7) She rechecks a cinch, and then lifts and stretches Pink Champagne's legs (8) to avoid discomfort from the girth.

(9) Members of the National Champion Leprechaun Team warm up. National Champion Sidney Stang and Kendel are coached by Joyce Post (10). Head and hand positions are important in vaulting; Kendel and Sidney practice a double Flag on the barrel (11). While Jeff Moore warms up Bobcat, Kendel also limbers up (12 & 13).

sweaty. We all found that very funny after the Kür had gone off so well. When we bowed and left the arena, we received a standing ovation. Once out of the ring, we all started talking at once about how the Kür had gone off so well. Later, at the awards assembly, we discovered ourselves the winners with a score of 7.447 and the next highest score was 6.2.

When the team got back from Germany, we were asked to do many demonstrations. We performed at a few fairs and at the Fest, but the Kür never went quite as well as it had in Germany. Most of the people who were on the team went for their gold medals when we got back. I didn't because I felt I was not ready, but I also wanted to get it with honors, so I waited.

The 1979 Fest, where I won my title, was the best yet. Ariana Fort and I were competing on the Leprechauns A team. We stayed down in Watsonville most of the summer and practiced with the team, vaulting twice a day, once in the morning and once in the evening. The coach, Joyce Post, was down there every day with us, lungeing the horse or writing our Kür. The Europeans were sending some teams over to compete with us, and Joyce wanted the A team to win the International Competition. We took several lessons from Jeff Moore. He helped us speed up our compulsories so we would have more time for the Kür. After Jeff had finished rearranging our Kür, it consisted mostly of triples (the judges like to see lots of difficult triples). What I like best about the way Jeff coaches is that he always has some new suggestion which usually works wonders on whatever your problem is.

The Fest finally arrived and it went great! The Leprechaun A team—Brian Post, Margie Cornell, Kim Gussenhoven, Ariana Fort, Jenny Cornell, Lisa Gussenhoven, Lisa Richardson and I—was super. We won the National A-team competition (first in compulsories and first in Kür), and we were International Reserve Champions. Individually our team did very well also. We had the Women's International Champion (me), first and third place National Silver Women (me and Ariana Fort), Silver Three-Phase Champion (me), Gold Three-Phase Champion (Kim Gussenhoven), Men's International Champion (Brian Post), and Men's Reserve International Champion (Kim Gussenhoven).

After the Fest I decided it was time I went for my gold medal. Brian and I were still silver medalists from our trip to Europe in 1977. We had always been a little bit competitive, so we both wanted to get a higher score on our medal exams. We took our tests and they went well for both of us—I had no idea who would get a higher score but assumed he would. We both passed our medal tests with honors, and the funniest part was that we got exactly the same score—9.701.

Since I earned my title I have been offered many opportunities. I gave numerous exhibitions (mostly with the

team I was on in 1979). I also was offered a spot in the next Rose Bowl Parade.

Vaulting has had its embarrassing moments. Once, when the Leprechauns were performing at the Santa Cruz Fair, I was about to do my dismount—a front flip. Jeff announced over the loud-speaker that I was the first American to do it, and after he had finished his little speech, I went for the dismount. Well, the next thing I remembered was overrotating it and landing face down in the dirt. I was so embarrassed I could have died, but instead I just lay there for a second, then picked myself up and ran over to the line. It seemed like everyone in the audience was laughing.

I ride, vault and do gymnastics. Sometimes I find it hard to do all three, but I always manage to find the time. I think being able to ride has been the greatest asset. My gymnastic ability has helped a lot, but not as much as my riding. So many times in vaulting you see a gymnast who has beautiful stretch and form, but just cannot perform on the horse because she has no sense of rhythm. When you know how to ride, it is so much easier to find the natural rhythm of the horse. Without rhythm you are working against the horse and can only get minimal height in most exercises. Also, working against the horse makes it hard to do even the basic moves. I can use the horse to my full advantage, so when I am trying some new exercise, I do not worry about whether the horse will be under me or not; if I just stick with the rhythm I will be all right.

(14-20) Kendel mounts her own horse, Hi Bebe, lunged by Inez. The Flag, which Kendel performs here (21), is one of the six basic exercises in vaulting competitions.

21

Vaulting on different horses used to be a big problem for me, but not anymore. When I was trying out for the U.S. team, I could barely stand on our own horse, let alone someone else's. Then Jeff and Inez made me stand on every horse available. I hated it at the time, but it sure worked wonders for my standing abilities. I have vaulted on different teams and with different people individually and I have to be able to adjust to their horses very

quickly. Now I can get on almost any horse and perform well.

More than anything my gymnastics have helped the way my vaulting looks. Being as limber as I am, I can get really good stretch in the exercises that need it, and when your leg is just as high as it can be, you always get better scores. I have been doing gymnastics seriously since seventh grade. I have competed on my school team twice,

and both years received a "most valuable" award in varsity gymnastics. Last year I went to the North Coast Sectionals—for the best school gymnasts in northern California. I was first on uneven bars and floor exercises (my two best events) and second on vault. I came in second all around. I have competed on a club team, which was very enjoyable because the level of competition was a little bit more difficult.

One of the most important things in vaulting is, of course, the horse. In countries where there are clubs just for this sport you find beautiful, trained horses that are kept in a special school, and that is a big advantage. But when vaulting is only part of the program it's not easy to

Another of the six compulsory exercises, the Flank, is demonstrated by Kendel on Bobcat (22-33).

34

find someone who will buy, keep and train a horse just for this.

It's best to learn vaulting on a cantering horse, because this gait has the easiest rhythm to follow, and it gives the learner a lift which helps him to do the exercises.

35

Before putting in very much time on training a horse for vaulting you should be sure that it has a well-balanced, slow canter which it can keep up without effort. Another important thing is that any horse used for this work should be very obedient on the lunge-line, because it is just no use trying anything with a horse until it is fully trained. The size of the horse is not too important. Most groups are mixed and it is really amazing how even quite little kids can learn to vault onto horses 15.3 hands high!

To have a good horse for vaulting the learners should make a fuss of him from the start, with lots of petting and handling, climbing all over him and giving him tidbits. It is very easy to see if the horse is going to object, and of course if it tends to kick when it is touched around the hind legs or bucks when the weight of a vaulter comes too far back, it must be rejected. Even beginning vaulters can

Kendel and two members of the Leprechaun Team perform (34) a triple exercise. Control of the cantering horse by the lunger (35) is very important. (36) Kendel and another team member perform doubles, the Flag and Cossack Hang.

help train a horse by getting him used to them at a standstill, and more advanced vaulters can start the training at the trot and then move up to a canter.

One of the hardest things to cure is the horse's tendency to slow down or stop whenever anyone runs towards him along the lunge-line or when anyone jumps off his back. This difficulty can be corrected by having the experienced vaulters get on at a standstill. Then the instructor starts the horse moving and has them vault off and run alongside the horse while the instructor concentrates on keeping it moving. When the learner can vault off at all gaits and run alongside, and the horse will keep its gait, the learner can start "running at him" to vault on.

So as not to be rough and frighten the horse while teaching him to let the vaulters run towards him, it is best to use the routine of beginning at the walk, then the trot,

40

and finally the canter. With the horse at the walk the vaulter stands at the instructor's side and then walks out along the lunge in step with the horse, to the horse's shoulder. With hands on the grips of the surcingle he walks along, keeping his shoulders parallel with those of the horse. When the horse will accept this and keep

41

walking along, he is then put at a trot and the vaulter repeats the procedure, always in step with the horse, trotting at the shoulder, holding on to the grips. And finally, the lesson can be done at a canter, the vaulter cantering on the same lead as the horse. Depending on the horse, this could take a couple of days or a week, and sometimes even longer. Lots of quiet patience is needed to produce the right result.

Since most people are right handed, vaulting is more easily done with the horse going to the left. It is sometimes helpful, though, for the learners to walk a while before going to the right, and it is really important for the horse to be either used part of the time on the right hand or be lunged on the right during his warm-up so he does not get too one-sided.

A horse can work for up to an hour at the standstill, walk or trot, but the limit should be about forty minutes when it is working mostly at the canter, and this includes rest between exercises. It is just as important to keep the

Kendel uses a number of dismounts, in this series of photographs (37-41), she demonstrates a back salto.

horse from becoming bored and irritated as it is to watch over his physical condition.

The equipment needed for vaulting is: a vaulting surcingle. It has a loop for the foot on the outside—or both sides (which is better but must be ordered specially), a ring on top with a stand-up rein, and rings on the side for fastening the side reins; a snaffle bridle; a lunge-line; side reins; and a lungeing whip.

The surcingle has to be well fitted, and padded on the withers—leather-lined padding is best. The grips must be

One of the most difficult individual Kür (freestyle) exercises is the flying split dismount (42-53).

54

sprung far enough out from the girth so the hand slips in and out easily without rubbing the knuckles. Rigid handles help the vaulter to lift himself over the horse better than the flexible ones do. A felt pad under the surcingle helps keep learners from slipping when they are practising (it is not allowed in competitions, but rosin can be used). A sheepskin cover to stop the horse being chafed is very useful and can be ordered with the surcingle.

For ordinary practice work a lungeing cavesson can be used with side reins attached to it. When the horse is used to being lunged on a snaffle bridle the reins can be done up out of the way through the throatlash, and the lunge-line is taken through the nearside bit ring, up over the head, and snapped to the off bit ring and the side reins attached. This way of fixing the lunge-line keeps its weight from pulling the bit through the horse's mouth. For competitions the reins are taken off the bridle and only the side reins are used. The lunge-line can also be run through the near side snaffle ring, under the chin, and snapped to the off side bit ring, or to a ring on a strap that connects the two bit rings.

Side reins are used to hold the horse's neck straight and to keep the head position as steady as possible, and in the rest periods the side reins should be undone.

I have been riding for almost thirteen years, and I still love horses. I have ridden many different horses. Some belonged to friends, others I sponsored. About two and a half years ago, I got my own horse named Cookie Cutter; she is a Quarter-horse and I show her Western. She was the first horse I looked at, and I instantly fell in love with her. When I got her she had very little training, so it makes me very happy to go to a show and do well, because I know I have put most of the training into her. Cookie is now seven and I plan to keep her forever!

I find it hard sometimes to do all the things I love, but I would not give up any of them. I figure my riding helps my vaulting; vaulting helps my gymnastics; and gymnastics helps my vaulting. To participate in three sports is tough, but they are at different times of the year, so that makes it a little easier.

I have been vaulting for five years now and have enjoyed every bit of it. It's too bad vaulting is not in the Olympics, it would be really exciting to compete. It used to be an Olympic event a number of years ago, but now there are not enough countries to participate, and it has been dropped. I am hoping to go to Europe again in

(54) Pink Champagne bucks, and the vaulters strain to keep their balance. International Men's Champion Brian Post, National Men's champion Kim Gussenhoven and Kendel perform the Triple Decker (55). (56) Brian and Kim support Kendel in the Flying Angel. Coach for the American team, Jeff Moore, and Elizabeth Searle, president of the American Vaulting Association, pose with Kendel and the awards the team brought back from Germany (57).

55

the Summer of 1981, but no sure plans have been made. I would really enjoy competing against the Europeans individually.

My parents were divorced a couple of years ago, but I did not have to quit vaulting; either Inez or my mother would take me to practice. My mother moved away and Dad remarried. Things were not working out so well at home, and I spent a lot of time away. When Inez Fort asked me if I would like to move in with her family, I accepted immediately. Even though I care greatly for both my parents, I feel right at home with the Forts.

I would say as a person I have a lot of shortcomings, but none that is really serious. I hate to be beaten at anything I do, I guess I have always been competitive. It is not so bad to be beaten if you have not been at the top; that always makes losing harder.

LUCINDA PRIOR-PALMER
england

*L*ucinda Prior-Palmer is the only horsewoman I have met who is a superstar in her own country. She was the last girl photographed for this book and I will not soon forget those early March mornings in England, especially one rainy morning at dawn, when I watched her galloping over the downs by Salisbury Plain.

In the words of the International Equestrian Federation (FEI): "The Three-Day-Event is the most complete combined competition, demanding of the rider considerable knowledge in all branches of equitation and a precise knowledge of his horse's ability, and of the horse a degree of general competence resulting from intelligent and rational training."

Horse Trials trace their origins to the tests devised for cavalry regiments, and on the Continent are still often referred to as the Military. Designed originally as a supreme test of fitness and courage for both horse and rider, the modern Event still retains these properties as its main objectives. Fitness to compete on three successive days in the three disciplines of dressage (to prove that the horse is educated, balanced and obedient to ride); speed and endurance and cross-country (involving twelve to fifteen miles of roads and tracks, steeplechase, and ultimately over thirty fixed natural obstacles to prove that the horse is both bold and clever and at peak fitness); and finally show jumping–comparatively simple compared with modern show jumping courses–designed, in this instance, to show that the horse is still fit to compete after the demanding cross-country phase; these are the elements that make up the sport of Three-Day-Eventing.

Great Britain is fortunate in its position as the major competitive Three-Day-Eventing country in the world, and the Three-Day-Event with most prestige is held each year in April at Badminton, the home of the Duke

Eventing superstar Lucinda Prior-Palmer with Killaire (1).

2

of Beaufort. Badminton is perhaps to Three-Day-Eventing what Wimbledon is to tennis or the Henley Regatta to rowing.

Lucinda Prior-Palmer's major achievement to date is that she is the only person to have won the Badminton Three-Day-Event on four occasions—and each time on a different horse. In 1973 on her own Be Fair, in 1976 on Mrs V. Phillips' Wideawake, in 1977 on Mrs H. Straker's George and in 1979 on Mr C. Cyzer's Killaire.

Now at the pinnacle of her sport, Lucinda's other major international successes are: European Champion 1975 on Be Fair; European Champion 1977 on George; and competed in the British Team in the Montreal Olympics 1976 on Be Fair.

In addition to these achievements, she has been the United Kingdom Three-Day-Event Points Champion on four occasions, and has been in the winnings consistently since 1973 on several different horses, an extraordinary achievement due entirely to natural talent, dedication and a lot of hard work!

Crossing Niagara Falls on a tight-rope, the artist loses his balance—he falls into the thundering torrent below. A pilot of the Red Devils aerobatic team fractionally mistimes a maneuver, gravity takes over, he plunges earthwards. A husband misjudges the balance between work and home life, his wife leaves. The Nazis upset the balance of power and the world was thrown into the turmoil of war.

At her home, Appleshaw House, Lucinda works Mairangi Bay in the dressage ring (2). Later (3), she takes him over a series of low jumps in a nearby wood.

3

Balance, timing, call it what you will, is a fundamental requirement in everything. From learning to walk to learning to deal with the life that comes our way, the better the balance the more successful the outcome. A lack of it may lead to falling off a stool, or to a tragedy, or it may lead to an international disaster.

Balance is hard to define, probably because it is very much subconscious. Everyone has it—some develop its capacity, others diminish it. In the main, it is guided by mental not physical attitude. It is this that I think explains why someone who is not a genius will often come out better than someone who is. He has to use more thought and greater effort to achieve even the level at which the genius begins. With such experience he may well discover the answer to more secrets than the genius who, because of his own abilities, has not had to apply himself to the same extent.

(4) Family pet, Oliver Plum, sits in one of Lucinda's trophies. Behind them can be seen some of her fourteen silver Badminton awards. (5) After an early morning work-out, Lucinda rides Beagle Bay along the road that passes through the village of Appleshaw. Lucinda with Killaire (6) in front of her house, and with Beagle Bay (7) at the stables behind the house. (8) The famous Killaire, the only horse to have been placed first, second and third at Badminton.

9

Frequently during the past eight years I have asked myself what exactly is the root of any success that I have been lucky enough to enjoy. Those who have tried to teach me will assure anyone that it is not genius. It is not high intelligence, nor unbounded talent. It is not money or intrigue. So why has success come my way? Great good fortune has been my lot in life. Time and again circumstance has reminded me that I was born under an exceptionally lucky star. The amazing heights have, inevitably, been well balanced by some galling lows, but all in all, I believe I am lucky, and I dread to think how I would cope if I believed I was unlucky.

Standing waiting with my horse at the start of the cross-country course of either an international Three-Day-Event, or a minor One-Day-Event, never ceases to scare me. Waves of self-doubt and the horror of the pending possibilities ahead, should my luck be having a day off, overwhelm me. It is then that I realize that it is something more than luck that I trust to. It is faith. Faith through communication; the communication shared with my horse, and to a more subconscious extent, with our maker.

How does a rider tell his horse what is ahead? In my imagination I see horse and rider as one big wheel, turning all the while. Through the rider's arms, down the reins, through the bit, through the horse's head and back down his neck, through his body, up through the rider's legs and the seat of his pants, and back down through his arms. Providing there are no missing links in the wheel, it is possible to communicate physical requirements to the horse; tricky fence ahead—shorten your stride and be ready to be quick and clever, or big, straightforward one ahead—just gallop on and throw a big easy jump.

At daybreak and in the rain Lucinda works out Beagle Bay on the downs near Salisbury Plain (9 & 10).

10

If the rider does not have the feeling of this continuously turning wheel then his horse is very unlikely to be in balance. Without a physical balance the horse will only be able to employ a part of his own abilities. It is the same for a sportsman in any sport—skiing, swimming, fencing and so on.

Putting a horse in balance and helping him to stay there comes easily to very few. One of my greatest strokes of luck, after the initial good fortune of being born to parents of such humanity, humor and intelligence as mine, was Be Fair.

Be Fair, a chestnut Thoroughbred, was my first horse. (Graduating from riding ponies to horses is somewhat akin to moving from roller skates to ice skates.) Be Fair had two indestructible assets: his heart and his incredible natural balance. He had to tolerate me from the age of fifteen years to twenty-two, and believe you me that was seven years of learning all the time for me, mostly by my mistakes. But for Be Fair, I would not be writing this piece now, because any of you who have heard of me

most certainly would not have done so without the Greatest, as our family came to know him.

He was a naughty, spoiled, five-year-old schoolboy when he first came to Appleshaw. Through good times and lean, we grew up in each other's company for the best part of seven years. Without me being fully aware of it, Be Fair developed in me a capacity to love that ventured far beyond my pony-mad instincts. All my childhood I had been smitten by horses and all to do with them, and I loved my three consecutive ponies to the exclusion of most schoolwork, and all homework. But to this initial and commonly-seen passion, Be Fair added another dimension—that of the building of a deep relationship based on mutual confidence and mutual respect. Eventually, so strong had the bond become that despite, at eighteen, being still in the kindergarten as far as the technicalities of the game are concerned, we won Badminton in 1973.

Lucinda and Charlie Micklem study the course at Shelswell where they will compete in a One-Day-Event the following morning (11) through (15).

Only too aware of my own inadequacies as a rider, I scribbled a poem after that unique occasion, and sat in fear and trembling waiting for my downfall.

Humbly he starts at the base,
Beginning his climb up and up
Onto and over the sturdy branches of experience.
Suddenly the world begins to notice a shaking of leaves
Some fall—others part
To make way for him.
Precariously balancing on a leaf at the top,
A leaf that will fall unhindered to the ground
When blown by that wind of ill-fate.

With such negative thinking and with a still very sparse knowledge of the intricacies of Three-Day-Eventing, the downfall inevitably happened. Struggling to learn to ride other horses, realizing that obviously Be Fair could not last forever, things started to go very wrong. In five major

international Three-Day-Events during the following two years, I registered five falls. One of them was even with Be Fair at the European Championships in Kiev, in the USSR.

My future was hanging in the balance when in the middle of 1975, an invitation to take Mrs Phillips' Wideawake to ride in the Boston Three-Day-Event at Ledyard Farm arrived. If I had one more fall at Ledyard, I had decided to quit—feeling ever more strongly that I was not worthy of the horses which carried me. They were good—it was I

who kept making the dreadful errors. Although we had been together for two years, Wideawake and I had not developed a hot-line of communication. A small connection was, however, made at Ledyard—we stayed on our feet. The relief was overpowering. I had not wanted to give up the life I had led for five years and the sport I was learning so much about.

The pendulum of favor continued to swing our way. Three months later, Be Fair romped across Luneburg Heath, to become Champion of Europe. The following

spring, Be Fair was excused Badminton, and saved for the Olympic Games in Montreal. Wideawake and I suddenly found our hot-line, literally as Badminton swung into motion. Together we won, and within minutes of victory, Wideawake died.

> Why so kind?
> Thank you.
> How privileged am I
> For all that you give me.
> The thrill of achievement
> Only surpassed by the thrill of communication.
> Just in time
> Why so kind?
> Just too late
> Would be most people's fate.
> Thank you, God, for such a find.

To this day, the cause of Wideawake's death is still a mystery. It was suspected that the vagal nerve slowed the excited action of his heartbeat as it is supposed to do, but then failed to remember to release its hold.

Three months later, Be Fair ended his competition days as he turned for the finish of the cross-country course at the Olympic Games and slipped his Achilles' tendon off his hock. He never, therefore, won the medal which he so deserved. Instead he won acclaim of a different sort.

So extraordinarily like a fairy tale was his life, until the hard truths of real life at its climax, that Be Fair's story made me try to write. So evolved *Up, Up and Away*—Be

Lucinda, her stable manager, Joanna Capjon, and Foxy Bubble wait for the dressage test to begin at Shelswell (16). After bowing to the judges, Lucinda and Foxy Bubble start their performance (17). Following the test she pauses to say hello to Captain Mark Phillips (18). With her mother (19) she walks from the dressage square toward her horse van to prepare for show-jumping.

Fair's biography. A medal would have only reflected a single triumph; a book reflected his whole career.

That was the end of Eventing the way I had always known and loved it. The core of the family, Be Fair, was no longer able to compete. His number two was in Heaven. The main back-up personality, my father, became very ill as, little by little, cancer took its hold.

Though it is only possible to know it in retrospect, 1977 was the start of an entirely new manner of existence. It happened to be the most successful year I am ever likely to have, but it was the year which was run off the mains. There was no longer the rustic, personal family feeling. The electricity was no longer generated by our own water-wheel at the bottom of the garden.

By a series of extraordinary circumstances, I was not without a horse to ride at Badminton, despite having lost both principal horses the previous year. Mrs Straker's George and Mr Cyzer's Killaire filled the gap. The former was a very good horse, but included, with his honest reputation, a string of falls. The latter was little more than a three-quarter Thoroughbred Irish hunter, who moved

(20) Before entering the show-jumping ring, Lucinda stops to have a word with her mother. Mairangi Bay and Lucinda taking some of the jumps (21-28). Both Mairangi Bay and Beagle Bay are young horses that Lucinda is training.

slower than the average hunter but employed such a time-saving manner of slithering over the fences that he had been runner-up at Burghley six months earlier, with us having been together then for only three weeks.

No one in our family had any confidence in either horse, but in their usual supportive and encouraging fashion they gathered together at Badminton. Outwardly, all was the same as usual. Daddy still played his back-up role as part groom and part coordinator. But no amount of his personal courage could disguise the inevitable.

Some time around the middle of the morning of cross-country day the mains took me over. Within thirty hours the unbelievable had happened. My father was able to witness the most improbable outcome of his last Badminton. George won and Killaire was third. He did not live to see George take the European Championships four months later, or Killaire come third in America, or Village Gossip make the runner-up in Holland.

None of the family really knew how any of these results came about. We were all living off the mains, in a numbed present, our own personal supply of generative power having steadied to a halt.

Both George and Killaire were horses with which I had had very little association before our combined confidence was put to the test. Fortunately, with both, the

hot-line was easy to find, unlike Wideawake or Village Gossip whose lines took years, not days, for me to discover. To this day, Village Gossip still keeps a little for himself. Even so, such was his tenacity across country, that our lack of communication in the first phase of the Three-Day-Event, the dressage, still left him runner-up at Badminton the following year, 1978.

That year we entered yet another sphere of attitude and existence. In order to compete, sponsorship was vital.

Overseas Containers Limited came forward with heartening generosity, enabling the financial worries of the past few years to be buried, at least temporarily.

A new pressure emerged, however. It could no longer be quite so funny if I lost the way or fell off, because now

Lucinda with Killaire (29) before starting the cross-country phase of the event. (30-36) Lucinda successfully negotiates jump eighteen on the Shelswell course.

With Mairangi Bay she goes over a double bounce, jump nineteen on the course (37-47).

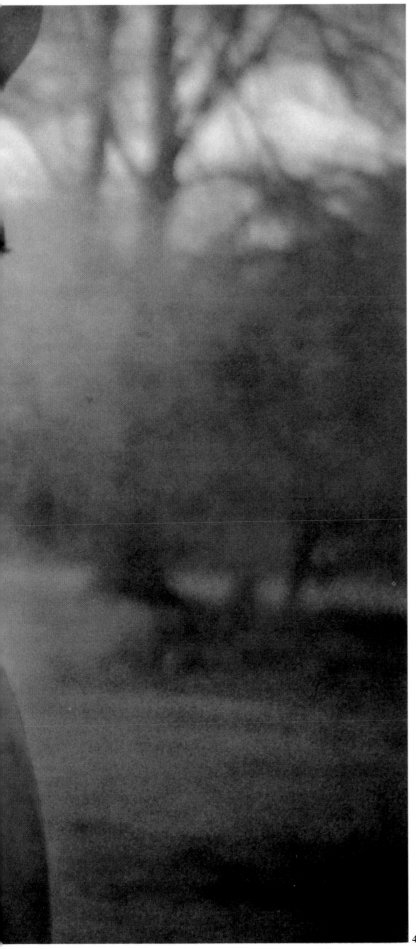

48

there was a company budget to answer for, not simply an enthusiastic and unselfish family with whom to laugh it off. To OCL's eternal credit, they never even applied a hint of pressure or displayed any displeasure. But the fact still remained that I was public property and had a duty to do a good job.

At times, so much of the family feeling and fun had vanished that I despaired of ever being able to explain to myself why I continued to Event. I would go away, usually abroad, during the off-season, for two months, and then I would know. After a welcome break it became increasingly difficult to live without that love, that joy of sharing and communicating, and the constant opportunity to learn something new.

There is a purity about that love, like a source of spring water. It is unselfish, undemanding, not possessive, spontaneous. Be Fair had led me through the natural human barrier to glimpse another dimension. When that glimpse is temporarily lost sight of, life seems very bare.

Since Be Fair's retirement in 1976 there has been one other man in my life, Killaire. Different from Be Fair in nearly every other way, he shares with him the same enormous heart and capacity to love, to trust, and to try. Killaire was never cut out to be an Event horse, and yet because of these qualities he has become a legend. The only horse to record first, second and third at Badminton, he won it in 1979, and this time it was he who motivated a desire to write another book, *Four Square,* a tribute to him—and to George, Wideawake and Be Fair—all of whom had a remarkable tale to tell of their individual Badminton victories.

My experience is only brief, but so far I have come to believe that communication is the balancing pole of life. Without it, one end of life outweighs the other and harmony, and therefore happiness, is impossible.

Lucinda and Killaire gallop away (48) from one fence and toward another at Shelswell. Having just finished the cross-country test, a proud rider praises her steaming horses (49).

49

NEENIE BLAKE

usa

T he editor of an American horse magazine had shown me the photograph of a girl dressed in white Indian costume, her arms outstretched, on the back of a bridleless, saddleless jumping horse. That photograph led me to Boise, Idaho, and Neenie Blake, queen of the Eh-Capa (Apache backward) Bareback Riders and Miss High-School Rodeo America.

To see the team formed by Jack, Alice and Neenie Blake—father, mother and daughter—in action was a delight. Jack takes care of the horses, their transportation and the heavy work that goes along with the rodeo. Alice is in charge of costumes and the dozens of other details. And Neenie supports and is supported by them both. Rarely have I seen such a united family effort.

Neenie had a special relationship with her horse, Buck. Having worked with her as a team for several years, Buck seemed to know what was expected of him. He also had a strong personality, which made him enjoyable and easy to photograph.

L ove of family is real and maybe taken for granted, and there is always a deep affection for pets such as dogs and cats, but a better companion than a horse is hard for a young girl to find. Memory is sometimes deceiving, but my first contact with horses was a ride with my father on a somewhat hyper family horse that belonged to some friends. This was not too long after my fourth birthday, my folks tell me. The infatuation may have begun with this ride; it is one of the few clear recollections of those years.

My eighth birthday was past before I rode a horse again. Dad, brother Mike, sister Leslie and I did some riding of rented horses in the foothills of California. Those stable veterans knew all of the tricks to pull on the inexperienced. These outings were infrequent, and I developed no affection for any special animal, but the desire had been born to have and ride a horse of my own.

(1) Miss High-School Rodeo America, seventeen-year-old Neenie Blake, dressed in her Eh-Capa costume, and her horse, Buck.

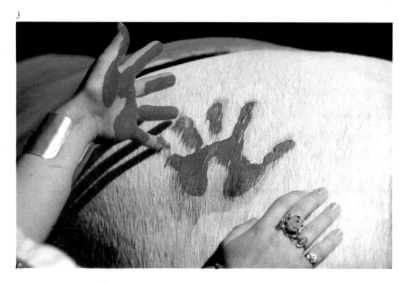

Dad's final Air Force assignment was to Maxwell Air Force Base, Montgomery, Alabama, where I had been born in 1963. Although the family talked horses during the trip there, there was to be no horse for me at that time. Pets became permanent members of our family, and as we had no experience moving something so big and active as a horse, we decided to settle on riding lessons for me, instead.

A stable run by a retired cavalry sergeant was selected for my sister and me. For me it turned out to be months in a circular corral with parallel fences arranged so that a horse could only go in one direction, except for turning around at the far end. This Hitchcock, as it was called, solved the problem of directional control, leaving the instructor free to concentrate upon each rider's control of gait and the correct seating for the particular maneuver being practiced.

All riding was English-style, and I must have learned some good basic habits, although at the time it didn't seem like I was advancing very rapidly. My sister progressed faster and moved to the intermediate level with beginning jumps in the big arena. The first time she fell off her horse, however, she lost interest in anything but riding for pleasure.

There were Field Days in which advanced students competed in hunter-jumper events against teams from other stables. As I watched, a desire to compete was growing in me, but it was not to be realized in Alabama. Father was retiring from the Air Force and we were heading for Idaho, where he had been raised, with a promise that I would have a horse.

One of the many horses we looked at was a kooky mare that seemed to settle down after Dad had ridden her for a while. She had been playing possum, however, and the first time she had a chance, she ran away with me. Seventy pounds was not enough to stop her, and she shied at a truck in the farmyard and dumped me into the truck bed. I woke up with my father driving me to the hospital. Mild concussion was not nearly as painful as the parental discussion about forgetting the horse business.

Polite insistence that I was all right won another chance, and the next weekend, a non-winning racehorse named Moonlight was mine. I spent a scary, cold winter trying to get that high-strung Thoroughbred to act like a pleasure horse. By spring she was reasonably pleasant to ride, but it took half the summer to get her to go into a horse trailer without a fight.

Neenie decorates Buck with feathers and handprints (2 & 3). Drillmistress Janice Southerland instructs the Eh-Capa Bareback Riders of Boise, Idaho (4). Neenie gallops Buck through the forest (5).

Queen of the Eh-Capa, Neenie does an Indian salute with the team (6 & 7), and then rides Buck through the group (8).

With a girl friend who knew about riding clubs, I tried out for membership in a drill unit called Eh-Capa Bareback Riders of Boise. Our apprentice season was a challenge. Moonlight's career lasted to mid-July, when she was drummed out of the troupe for taking part in a kicking fight as our group was parading in downtown Salinas, California. Fortunately, only the horses suffered any injury. Moonlight stayed in California to heal up and to be bred to a Thoroughbred stallion. The last half of the performance year was spent riding borrowed horses, which tested anew my riding skills and dedication.

Joining the Chickasaw Choctaw 4-H Club early that year added other dimensions to my horsemanship. It taught me horse care, grooming, the basics of showmanship and competitive-event riding. My first ribbon, a fourth place, was won on Moonlight, which really kindled a competitive urge, but with Moonlight retired, a new horse was needed for the next year in Eh-Capa. Coming up was the 4-H competition at the fair and a contest for Eh-Capa Junior Princess. Just when it appeared that these events would have to be missed, the Queen of the 4-H

13

14

Without saddle or bridle, Neenie takes Buck over a jump in an exercise that has made the Eh-Capa riders famous (9-12). The team (13) does the jump which in (14) is executed in opposite directions by Neenie and Janice.

12

Club, Jackie Collins, introduced me to a gray horse she had used in Eh-Capa and 4-H in previous years. She and her mother had trained him and were looking for a new owner who would use his skills and give him a good home. Jackie had selected me to be Buck's new owner.

Dad was hesitant because we had not been very successful with Moonlight. Buck was brought to the fairgrounds, where Jackie taught me how to cue him for the many things he was trained to do. We convinced my folks that he was the horse and that he would be ready for the Fall events. Buck, in his many roles, is the horse pictured in these pages. He is part of my life, my winner, babysitter to my nephews, provider of quiet rides for the inexperienced and meek, and appropriately spirited rides for the bold.

There were ribbons and honors with Buck from the very beginning in 4-H, and he started me on my queen quests by helping me become second runner-up in the Eh-Capa Junior Princess Contest a few weeks after we found each other.

As I learned to get more and more from Buck, success followed success. The next season we were in the jump line with the experienced Eh-Capa members and some of the select few who could perform in the Liberty routine,

Neenie and Buck repeat the same jump in an Idaho forest (15 & 16).

in which horses are ridden with a strap around the base of the neck. Liberty comes after the main act. The Liberty horses enter the arena, where the last vestige of control, the strap around the neck, is removed and maneuvers are performed in unison, control exercised only by voice and leg.

At the next fair Buck made me Grand Champion Showman, and in succeeding years in Eh-Capa we advanced together, until in 1979 I was queen and he was the solo highjump horse.

There has been anguish with Buck. He suffers from the gray horse syndrome—malignant tumors. In 1977 the first one, about duck-egg size, was removed from the sheath area. There have been several small soft-tissue and surface growths removed since then. He always recovers and carries on as he did for the photographs in this book, just one month after the last batch had been removed.

The extensive Eh-Capa association with professional rodeos and some participation in Little Britches and 4-H speed events led naturally to High-School Rodeo. My parents have supported whatever I felt I was capable of doing with horses. They foot the bills and actively support me without pushing. When I mentioned High-School

Rodeo, they left it up to me. I joined the first year I was eligible, but confined participation to barrel racing, pole-bending and goat tying. I didn't qualify for state in any of these events, but I did observe much of the queen contest and had an idea how it was conducted for the district.

The urge to be queen had been with me since placing third in the Eh-Capa Junior Princess Contest my first try. I was determined to be Eh-Capa queen someday. Talking to former queens, I slowly began to realize that there was a lot more to queening than just riding a horse. My next try, I was first runner-up for junior princess, but I still wasn't prepared in all the needed skills. Fortunately, though, by this time the family was collecting and cataloguing bits of information that could be useful when preparing for a queen competition.

All of us had accepted the fact that rodeo queens are not born, they must be developed. I attribute my success to long-range planning and hard work. Like everything else in our society, rodeo-queen contests have become increasingly competitive. The time had come to take stock. My riding skills were improving, and I had a Quarter horse that was a proven reining horse, and had proved to be a queening horse when lent to a friend who won a queen contest with him. With Buck for Eh-Capa and another horse for rodeo queening, I needed to continue to improve my own ability to work with horses. What really needed improving was a fourteen-year-old girl. There was no question about the main goal. Eh-Capa was it.

Christine Doherty, Miss Rodeo Idaho 1975, was supervising a queen clinic for the local district of High-School Rodeo, and she suggested my mother and I attend. This was an eye-opener to the many techniques and skills needed in this game. I really worked hard at this clinic, and remember the butterflies in my stomach when I had to model and to give my speech. With newfound confidence and poise, the junior princess title was mine the next fall; princess of my 4-H Club followed in a week. Training was beginning to pay off.

I was still tiny but had grown enough so my mother began to buy clothes from former queens to be altered for me when the time came to compete at rodeos. I attended a second district-queen clinic in the Spring of 1978, and the Eh-Capa competition that fall resulted in my selection as queen.

Eh-Capa queens traditionally compete in at least one local rodeo contest, so fall and winter were frantic. I attended a self-improvement and modeling school to perfect makeup, hair styling and modeling skills. I took two semesters of speech training, worked on my Eh-Capa

Neenie in one of her rodeo costumes (17). (18 & 19) She and Buck barrel race, a rodeo event in which the contestants, each trying for the shortest time, ride around three barrels in a clover-leaf pattern.

queen costume and stood for endless fittings as out fits were adjusted to my size in anticipation of July competition at a local summer rodeo. Also, I had to study rodeo rules and event leaders of the past and present, understand current events and the news and attend, once again, a district-queen clinic in the Spring of 1979.

The decision to compete in the 1979-1980 District II Queen Contest, although two months away, mobilized the family. Dad began to help condition the horses. Mom, the wardrobe mistress, was up half the night and, with the help of two very dear friends, completed the tedious job of reconstructing clothes to a skin-hugging fashion. There were matching boots to dye and belts to make; scarves, hats, gloves and accessories were tried, compared and modified for each outfit before passing inspection. Saddle pads were hand made out of rug material and bound in leather to match each outfit.

I was very busy perfecting a two-minute speech, practicing modeling, working on horsemanship and studying, studying, studying—everything from current events to the minute detail of each and every page of the High-School Rodeo Rule Book. Mom was my coach; Dad criticized my delivery and every movement of my head, eyes and hands. I gave my speech over and over again. It was taped and replayed to correct any minor defect that could be amplified by an audio system.

It was hard work and I had other responsibilities to meet. As president of the Idaho Junior Quarter-horse Association, I had to help organize a stallion service auction in January to provide support for the Idaho team at the world finals. There was a June Quarter-horse show to

In goat tying, Neenie rides Buck into the arena (20), dismounts and runs toward the goat (21), throws it (22) and ties its legs (23) in the shortest time possible (24).

23

manage. I needed to appear and compete in as many youth shows as I could, and there were the correspondence and other details of the association. As 4-H Club President, I had many of the same kind of responsibilities on a lesser scale.

The Eh-Capa queen must practice with the troupe repeatedly to ensure proper leadership and the refinement of new routines. Janice Southerland, the drillmistress, was one of my best supporters and had helped me over the years as I was learning the skills required of a queen. She made it possible for me to meet the involved schedule of High-School Rodeo with minimum disruption to any Eh-Capa duties.

Time slipped by as each remaining discrepancy assumed panic proportions, no matter how minor it appeared in relation to the total effort. Finally, no more could be done—the time had come to put more than three years of preparation to the test. There were new speeches to prepare and the same pressures were repeated, as the state queen contest was only six weeks away.

With the state title won, only three weeks remained before the national finals. A major problem was to find a cutting horse to compete on at the finals in Fargo, North Dakota. Finally, Max Roberts of Mountain Home, Idaho, agreed to let me use the cutting horse which his grandson was going to use in boys' cutting. With this arranged, I concentrated on current events as my mother worked long hours altering clothes, and Dad fed and took care of the horses and prepared for the trip to North Dakota. Soon we were at the finals and the ten days of competition began.

The final day arrived and the queen contestants all made their high-speed entry and lined up. Awards were announced for horsemanship, congeniality and queen runner-ups. My name had not been called. At last the announcer said: "And now the new National Queen from the high-mountain country, Miss High-School Rodeo Idaho—Neenie Blake."

My reign so far has been an exhilarating experience. When it is over, my youth and the age requirements of

professional rodeo queening will give me two or three years for competitive riding events and to prepare skills for future queen competition—maybe someday to represent Idaho in the Miss Rodeo American Contest.

There have been other horses in my life as well as Buck. Repent, a stocky, sorrel Quarter-horse gelding, excels at reining, working cowhorse and high-speed buzzing for rodeo queening. Sandy, a palomino Quarter-horse, who weighs almost 1,500 pounds, is a steady performer in both English and Western events and won the Junior Quarter-horse Thirteen-and-Under All-Around title for me his first year of competition. My new filly in training, a Quarter-horse called Deebars Shady Lady, was lost to an injury after these pictures of Buck were taken.

There have been other moments of pain associated with my horses, such as the first realization that Buck's

In pole bending, another rodeo event (25-30), Neenie must weave in and out of a line of poles without knocking any down, and as fast as she can.

29

28

27

26

tumors were malignant; he is a member of the family and will be with us until he dies. There was the anguish and loss when Moonlight had to be put down because of a broken leg. These big events are loosely connected with the little moments when a horse is hurt—I hurt with them—and the doctoring which follows. It is particularly difficult for me to give them shots, and I try to get Dad to do this as well as dress wounds when necessary. Even though I know the treatment is necessary, I still don't care to be the one to hurt a horse in any way.

As I begin to pass on the crowns I have possessed for a year, it still seems a little unreal. I am still competing in

Neenie among some of her ribbons and trophies (31). (32) The diamond-studded National High School Rodeo crown. (33) Neenie with her father and mother. The back of one of the saddles that Neenie has been awarded (34).

other events, and I recently won the district girls' cutting with another of Max Roberts' horses, Coke. My intention is to rodeo all the way to the finals in Yakima, Washington.

I have been asked to train young girls and to school horses, but time is not available now—maybe later. This year I put on the district-queen clinic more or less by myself, with my mother as support. The transition from being one of the crowd to a recognized leader has been exhilarating and somewhat demanding. I am just now beginning to realize what has occurred as aspiring queens seek my advice.

But it all started with a casual meeting, as most love affairs seem to do. It has grown with each horse I meet, but Buck still has a select spot in my heart because he raised me through my beginning years. I cannot think of a more fitting tribute for any of the horses I love than these pages.

MERCEDES GONZÁLEZ
spain

*T*he first time I ever saw a horse worked on the long reins was several years ago in Jerez de la Frontera when the Spanish Riding School of Vienna was performing in Spain. That white stallion seemed like some marvelous automated porcelain toy. Even more impressive were the maneuvers of the rider, dismounted and walking behind the animal, his chest barely inches from its tail, his feet in perfect coordination with its hooves and matching them stride for stride, and later controlling the stallion's spectacular Caprioles and Courbettes with a deft touch on the rein.

More recently, while watching a similar performance by Alvaro Domecq's Andalusian School of Equestrian Art, I was surprised to see a girl among the riders. Riding in southern Spain is very much a male preserve. Later when the tall, dark, fine-featured girl dismounted to work a stallion on the long reins, it was easy to see why even the most rigid prejudice could not have faulted her performance. When it came time to select a young woman to represent Spain in this book, Mercedes González was the obvious choice.

In the late Fall of 1979, I visited Mercedes at her father's house in the village of Alcocer, near Madrid, to take pictures of her training her Portuguese and Spanish stallions. There, and later in Jerez de la Frontera, I became more and more impressed by her skill as a horsewoman, both in the saddle and working with the long reins.

"You can see," she once said to me, "that if it took brute force to train horses I could never handle them. But muscle isn't needed—head and heart are the absolute necessities."

Mercedes González has since been accepted as a student by the Spanish Riding School of Vienna—one of the greatest honors for any rider, man or woman.

*I*t is not easy to explain how I fell in love with horses and why my life has revolved around them; certainly no one else in my family is a dedicated rider.

(1) Mercedes González of the Andalusian School of Equestrian Art with a Spanish stallion.

I was born in Madrid twenty-six years ago, and when we were small children my parents sent my brothers, my sister and me to have riding lessons. But it was not till I was seven and was sent to boarding school in England that my attention became fixed on riding. I have wonderful memories of riding English ponies. It took me some time to overcome my fear, especially when the pony made a movement I didn't know how to control; but as time passed, my fear gradually disappeared and I began to feel more secure and able to enjoy all the pleasures of riding.

When, at the age of fourteen, I went to school in Madrid, my father began to take charge of my riding. He took me to the country club for lessons, where there was a large group of boys and girls of my age who also rode

(2) Mercedes calling the Andalusian stallion, Senador, to her (3). Senador being led (4) to a field. Mercedes lunges Senador (5-16) whose first frisky leaps will soon give way to controlled action.

and, like me, hoped one day to have their own horses. When he saw how keen a rider I was and how happy it made me, my father began to think about buying me a horse.

By chance he saw an advertisement in a newspaper for "well-trained horses." This immediately aroused his curiosity—in Spain horses are never sold by advertisement. This was how we met José Antonio García Gans. Gans took my father and me to a military barracks where he stabled his horses, although he was a civilian. He was a very friendly, open man and very important to me. When he saw how much I loved horses, he helped me from the very first day.

Later Gans introduced me to dressage. He helped me so much and taught me so many things that soon I realized that dressage was a much more enjoyable form of riding, and I gave up jumping completely to devote myself to this new form of equestrian discipline. Gans also lent me horses so that I could take part in competitions, and before long I was taking dressage lessons from Mary Allen, an Englishwoman, who was also teaching my father and my brother. With her help I continued to improve and to take part in more difficult competitions.

When Mary had to return to England, I felt lost without my teacher, but fortunately I also knew the type of work my horse needed, thanks to her lessons. It was then that my father, feeling that I had not advanced sufficiently and because we couldn't find a teacher in Madrid, decided to

send me and my mare to Jerez de la Frontera in April 1974, to begin a completely new phase in my equestrian life.

When I arrived in Jerez I was taken into my aunt María Dacia's house, and although she had eight children, she treated me as a daughter. My mare was kept at the polo club, where only one rider practiced dressage.

A few days later, on my father's instructions, I went to call on Alvarito Domecq. Alvarito, as well as fighting bulls

Mercedes rides (17 & 18) her Lusitano stallion, Leiria, through fields near her home, and later through the streets of Alcocer (19).

from horseback, and breeding horses and fighting bulls, had formed an equestrian show with a few friends after winning the Spanish Ministry of Information and Tourism's Golden Horse award. He continued his show with the idea of creating a school of equitation, somewhat similar to the one in Vienna, but with Andalusian horses. The show had been operating for less than a year and it was already quite popular and well known. Alvarito, having made a large investment in it, had rented a building in which to give performances.

The Spanish walk demonstrated by Leiria (20-23).

The show was made up of displays of Andalusian country riding, dressage, hand work and High Movements. At this time classical dressage was almost unknown in Andalusia, but thanks to the school it was becoming more popular.

I arrived one morning at the school and although there were a lot of people there, I quickly realized who Alvarito was and introduced myself. After watching the training for a while, I left. A few days later I went back, riding Gazhi. This time Alvarito invited me into the ring and watched me working the mare. Afterward he invited me to lunch to meet the other riders, among whom were another bullfighter, Manuel Vidrié, and a breeder of horses and bulls, Javier García Romero. Following lunch, Alvarito, having questioned me a little about my equestrian knowledge, asked me if I would like to come to the school to give lessons to the riders. I was very surprised. I thought I must have misunderstood and asked him to repeat his question. He did. After thinking a little I explained that I didn't consider myself capable yet of giving lessons, and refused his offer.

A month or so later my father came to Jerez and, in front of Alvarito, told me that I ought to give lessons at the school. So, at my father's request, I presented myself the next day to begin teaching, and thus became a member of the school. For the first few months I taught only the beginners, but my horse was kept at the school to make things easier for me.

After a few months of teaching, I went with Alvarito to his father's house to see a dappled Andalusian colt he had bred. I saw it for the first time in its stall, and, in spite of its long, thick tail and a mane that came almost to its knees (very characteristic of Andalusian horses), it looked big and clumsy. However, in the ring the colt changed completely; its movements were unusually

well-balanced for a horse of its age, and after galloping around it began to do the most spectacular extended trot. I was very surprised because it is rare in a Spanish horse and it was fascinating to see. Alvarito offered it to me to train, and I didn't hesitate a moment in spite of its looks and its inauspicious name, Odioso, which means hateful. I soon learned that his mild character, his willingness to work and his good manners were unlimited. A few days later he was brought to the school and I realized that I had been given the horse because no one else wanted him. But my expectations were never disappointed.

Sometime afterward Alvarito decided that I should take part in the show when it went to England, and with this in mind he bought a bay horse, whose name, curiously enough, was Gazhy, especially for my part in the show. He also designed a new number for me so that the rest of the show need not be changed, and thus the Pas de Quatre, or School Movements, came into being.

After several months' training I made my debut at Wembley Stadium in London, where the school gave several performances before going on to Paris for more shows. In spite of the responsibility of giving this type of public performance, I always felt sure enough of myself never to lose my calmness or feel nervous before going on—perhaps because of having taken part in so many riding competitions.

Back from London the work continued every morning. A Portuguese rider, Francisco Cancella, had joined the school and became a great help to all of us. With his assistance I began to realize clearly what I was capable of in my work and to what extent I was dedicated to horses.

That spring Alvarito took Gazhy home to teach him bullfighting. The last time I showed him was during the Jerez Horse Fair, which takes place every year at the beginning of May. The Spanish Riding School of Vienna came to give some exhibitions, and both schools did a show together. After that Gazhy went bullfighting and no longer took part in the show.

Meanwhile my own mare, Gazhi, had been sent to the country to be bred. It seemed doubtful whether I could continue at the school with only one horse, and I tried to persuade Alvarito to sell me Odioso, but he wouldn't.

After some six months without performing in the show, Alvarito decided I should return to it; he had been offered a contract for Holland and Belgium. A search began for a horse to replace Gazhy, and soon I went with Francisco to look at a Portuguese stallion named Leiria. We went back to tell Alvarito about him, believing he would be suitable. Although he was only five, he had already been taught the Piaffe and the Passage, performing them with great ease and polish. He also had a most spectacular extended trot. Alvarito got in touch with the owner with the idea of buying the horse, but he never did.

Leiria's extended trot (24-28); the Piaffe (29) and Passage (30).

28

31

32

Having no horse of my own to ride, I thought it would be a good idea to buy the Portuguese horse myself. As I was keen on it, Benito Fábrega, who is now my husband, agreed to come and see it, and ended by buying it and giving it to me as a present. In February Leiria arrived at the school, looking slightly changed. He had lost quite a lot of weight on the long journey, and it took some time for him to regain it because he had to work really hard to prepare for the school's shows abroad. When Leiria joined the school, I was asked to choreograph a new act for the Pas de Quatre, and I also designed something new for the Carrousel Gallop, although this last number was reserved exclusively for the men.

After practicing for little more than a month, we left for Holland and Belgium, taking part in the horse trials at Hertogenbosch and performing in Brussels. The school had a huge success, but for the horses the long trip in trucks was hard and the change of climate disastrous. Leiria had health problems the whole time we were away; I had to refuse to let him take part in the last shows. After this trip the school stayed in Spain and began to do shows all over the country. The shows improved technically each time, and the tension between the riders, which was caused by nerves, began to disappear.

When I had been working two years in the school without a holiday, I told Alvarito that I wanted to go to

With other members of the Andalusian School of Equestrian Art, Mercedes waits for a performance to begin (31 & 32). The quadrille performs in Jerez de la Frontera, where it was founded by Alvaro Domecq Romero (33-35).

my family at Alcocer the following summer and take Leiria with me. From then on I went home for a month every summer, taking Leiria and whichever horses I might have been assigned at the time, and I was able to have a holiday without interrupting my horses' training.

Every July a group of new colts would arrive at the school to be broken. Alvarito shared them one to each rider. Five months after being assigned Odioso, I was given a Spanish colt. Now and then I did ride other horses for short spells until they were assigned to other riders. The great variety of horses I rode both inside the school and out was an invaluable experience.

I think the main reason I wasn't given more horses was that in Spain it is very rare for a woman to ride every day, and even rarer for her to train horses; and so there was a lack of confidence in my horsemanship. This is clearly indicated by the fact that during the early years my salary was merely symbolic, less than those of the other beginners. I was never called by my name but simply referred to as "the girl," and whenever I asked for something they didn't want to give me, the excuse was always that I was only there for fun. This, no doubt, was good for me, but I have never understood why I was admitted to a school almost exclusively reserved for men.

Isabel Karanitsch, with whom I had become friendly when she came to Jerez because of her interest in horses, invited me several times to stay with her in Vienna. Thanks to the friendship of members of the Spanish Riding School there, I was able to watch their training and to ride with one of them, Arthur Kottas. His lessons and the talks I had with him made me realize the importance of aesthetics; of riding with elegance and ease to give the impression that riding is very simple and comfortable. I spent many mornings watching the work at the Viennese school, and followed attentively the High Movements and the training with long reins.

The Passage on the long reins demonstrated by Mercedes and the Spanish stallion, Garboso (36 & 37).

43 42 41

44 45 46

I became very interested in hand work. My first success at this was the Piaffe in hand with Leiria. For me it was like being the conductor of an orchestra—when he lifts his baton the music begins. When one gestures with the whip, the horse begins to dance. Leiria later went on to do the Piaffe between pillars, and he obeyed me though I was quite a distance from him. It is a great feeling to see a horse dancing, completely under one's control, almost without having to do anything.

(38-46) Mercedes and Garboso execute a pirouette in canter on the long reins.

A new rider now joined the Jerez school, Luis Ramos Paul, who was already famous, having four times won the Championship of Spain in Spanish Country Riding. At first, he only took part in the country-riding numbers, but because he was already well acquainted with dressage, he soon began to ride in the other numbers.

In November 1977 the school appeared for the first time in Madrid, with great success, and on our return to Jerez, I was allowed to use the long reins. These reins enable a horseman to execute all the School Movements and figures while dismounted. The work needs a special ability; it is difficult to keep a really delicate touch on the

47

48

49

50

51

52

Mercedes trains a stallion for the Capriole (47-53).

horse's mouth at such a distance. It was almost impossible for me not to interfere with the horse's movements at first, and it took time to learn to be gentle enough and to move in concert with the horse, but finally I learned to work in rhythm.

Once I was given the long reins, I was assigned a horse, which had been broken by a rider who had since left the school, to teach it the Capriole. This movement, where the horse gives a strong kick with its hind legs while in the air in full leap, is considered the most important leap of all and in the past was used in wartime to scatter foot soldiers. It is not an easy movement, and is even less so

It will take hours of training before this stallion's Capriole is perfected (54 & 55).

when the horse has already shown a disinclination to be-ing trained. When I was practicing the movement, I sometimes doubted I would ever get it right. I was starting with a horse that had already been wrongly taught and would only give a forward, uncontrolled leap. I had to practice quite alone. Normally the airs about the ground

are performed by two riders, but no one would put themselves under my orders, and so it was unlikely that I would ever succeed.

I used up a great deal of patience and a great many sugar lumps, and I was very careful not to let the horse es-cape me during the execution of the leap and to make him pay strict attention to my directions. Once when he was doing the Capriole close to the wall, I began to direct him from behind, standing in the center of the ring, but he was very difficult and kept crossing in front of me so

(56) Mercedes, working in hand, primes a horse for the Courbette. She executes the same maneuver while mounted (57).

At fiestas Spanish horsewomen wear flamenco dresses and ride sidesaddle (58), or sit on a pad behind the rider (59).

putting its forefeet to the ground. It is a very pretty leap, but the rider must be able to hold himself in the saddle with his legs without depending on the reins, so that he does not slip back when the horse leaps. Otherwise even though the horse does not fall backward, the center of gravity is lost and it becomes clear that the horse's leap is uncontrolled.

Back in Jerez I began on the Mounted Capriole. At first it seemed too fast and violent, and my directions always a second too late. I needed all my sensibility not to distract the horse with my hands, legs or crop as he leaped, but I soon felt completely at ease in this jump.

That October I went to live in Madrid with my husband, but continued to practice at the school. In November I went with the school to Argentina. On my return I left Leiria in Jerez so that Alvarito could continue to use him in the show. Of the seven horses I had been riding I took three that had not yet performed in public to Madrid: a four-year-old, a five-year-old and Odioso, who, although he had learned everything, had hardly ever been ridden in a show. He was the only horse I was allowed to ride continually during my time with the school. When he had learned to do all the movements of the Grand Prix, I began to practice the Spanish Walk, the Canter on the Spot, and various Pirouettes at the canter. I can't describe my enjoyment as I rode him both in training work and in the country. He had a heart of gold and enough qualities to satisfy any rider—his manners, good behavior and elegance charmed everyone who rode him while he was with me, and he always showed intelligence, delicacy and understanding.

Many people speculate on the ideal character of the Spanish horse. These days more emphasis is given to its looks and beauty than to its usefulness, and to a great extent the Spanish horse has become a drawing-room horse. It is now used mostly as a carriage horse, trained to take short paces and to lift and wing its forefeet.

Since it began, the Jerez school has tried to promote the Spanish horse as a riding horse, which it originally was. All the great riders of the past have praised its qualities, and it was the most popular mount until the last century, perfect both for show riding and as a warhorse. Its main characteristics are strong, solid legs, a powerful, graceful neck, a broad chest, a rounded rump, and an abundant mane and tail. Its head is expressive and beautiful, with a straight or convex nose. Its agility, flexibility and grace, its showiness, spirit and above all its docility (although it is never gelded), are outstanding.

In 1980 I continued to train at the school, but I didn't ride in any shows. Finally, I took my own horses to Madrid, but had to leave behind the ones that belonged to the school, including my dear Odioso. Never will I forget the times I spent in Jerez, for my horseman's spirit and my heart are still there.

that his hooves would hit me when he kicked out with his hind legs. Then he began to play up as he did the Capriole, and I had to correct him when he jumped without orders. But when at last I got him under control, I had the most marvelous feeling as he leaped before me in such spectacular style, with so little effort on my part.

In June 1979 we were sent to Venezuela, where I presented the Mounted Courbette. In the Courbette the horse rears back on its haunches and gives several leaps without

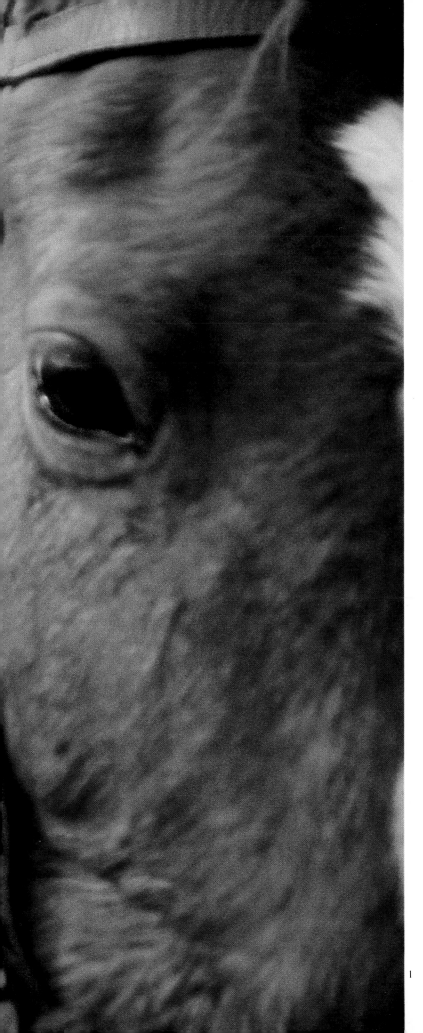

CINDY FOLKERSON

usa

"*It* has to hurt," I thought each time I sat in a movie theater and watched horses falling. Never would I have imagined there are horses that seem to love falling until I met a twenty-year-old mare called Flozac and a Hollywood stunt girl named Cindy Folkerson.

Flozac is owned by a stunt man, Carl Pitti, and when I saw her she was being worked by Cindy at Carl's ranch near Hemet, California. Cindy's father was a famous stunt man, and as a child she had occasionally worked in films but had only recently decided on a career as a stunt woman. Cindy had not had a lot of experience falling horses, so she welcomed the opportunity to practice with Carl's mare.

Jeff Ramsey, Cindy's husband, was on hand with Carl to coach her. One part of the team, though, needed no coaching–the mare seemed delighted with the idea of falling. After Cindy had practiced four or five times, it was difficult to keep the mare on her feet. No sooner was Cindy back in the saddle than Flozac would try to fall, giving rise to some very comical situations.

Stunt work takes courage, and Cindy has it. The last time I saw her was in Hollywood on the set of Charlie Chan and the Curse of the Dragon Lady. *The script called for Cindy to ride up to the camera, rear the horse and fall off. The director called for quiet, and while dozens of technicians prepared their lights, cameras and sound equipment, I asked Cindy, just as she got into the saddle, "How many times have you done this trick in the past?" Smiling nervously, she answered, "Never," and rode off.*

My family has always been horse oriented. Before I was born my father, Bob Folkerson, had a ranch where the Los Angeles International Airport now sits. He raised horses and cattle and grew alfalfa, at the same time

(1) Hollywood stunt woman Cindy Folkerson and twenty-year-old stunt mare Flozac.

2

traveling the rodeo circuit and working as a stunt man. By the time I was born, we ranched land in Torrance, California, and also belonged to a private club in Rolling Hills Estates called The Empty Saddle Club.

I was about three years old when I first started riding. My father and brother were team ropers, and during the ropings Dad would let me follow the cattle down to the end of the arena on his horse. Well, I was always fine going down, but once I got there Flashy Bob would stop and stand and I couldn't get him back up to the chutes. I was little and I'd kick with all my might, but he wouldn't feel it. So I'd holler for Dad, and he'd come and rescue me.

I was extremely small and frail. My sister and I both looked as if we would break if we did anything hazardous, but we used to do crazy things. We would ride double, facing the tail of Samba, the horse we had as kids. This was when I fell my first horse (accidentally). Patsy and I were bouncing along at an extended trot when I started to lose my balance and fell off. I didn't let go of my sister and pulled her off on top of me. She, in turn, pulled the horse on top of her. If I did that as a stunt today, I would make a bundle of money. Unfortunately, that one was for free.

(2) Cindy and Flozac start their run. (3-5) Cindy drops the left rein while pulling on the right to bring the mare down (6).

15

16

115

My father trained his own falling horses for motion pictures. Quite often when I was riding them, I unknowingly cued them and they would just fall over. I would step off and yell for my dad to rescue me once more. Around the time I was eleven, my brother (who is ten years older than me) set aside his rope and began riding jumping horses. I idolized him; he was the world to me. So, like brother, like sister, I had to do the same. He showed jumpers and I would groom for him. I showed hunters.

Naturally, as I grew up around the motion-picture industry, it wasn't a big deal. When I turned eighteen, my father wanted to get me my union cards (Screen Extras Guild, Screen Actors Guild); but I wasn't interested. Riding was something I did for pleasure. My career was commercial art. At this time I was attending Los Angeles Art Center and doing some free-lance artwork. I never considered working as a stunt woman. My father had enough insight to put me in the unions anyway. It's extremely difficult to get in; and if you're not a member of the union, you can't get work.

Flozac, who is helped up by Cindy (17, 18 & 19), appeared hardly able to wait for another fall.

In 1975 I began working as an extra. Extras are the people you see in television and films who walk around in the background and have silent parts. They may interact with the actors, but they don't speak. I worked with my father in a show called *Oregon Trail* (he drove a covered wagon). We worked on that show about three weeks at a ranch in Agoura, California. I was still attending school at this time. After the filming of *Oregon Trail,* my dad became ill with cancer. He died six months later. It was at this time that I dropped out of college and started working more in television as an extra.

Working as an extra was great training. I learned a lot about the technical end of the business and became more comfortable in front of the cameras. At the same time, I watched the stunt people work and began meeting people who could help me develop my career. It was very frustrating at first. I had reached the point where I knew what I wanted to do but didn't know quite how to go about it. Oh, how I missed Dad. I needed his help and guidance, but it was too late.

What helps me get jobs is being "Bob Folkerson's daughter." People assume since he was handy, I will be too. Once that gets me on the job, it's up to me to prove I

Cindy is made up to double actress Melissa Gilbert (20) on the set of Little House on the Prairie. *Now dressed alike, Melissa and Cindy pose with the horse that will be used in the stunt (21).*

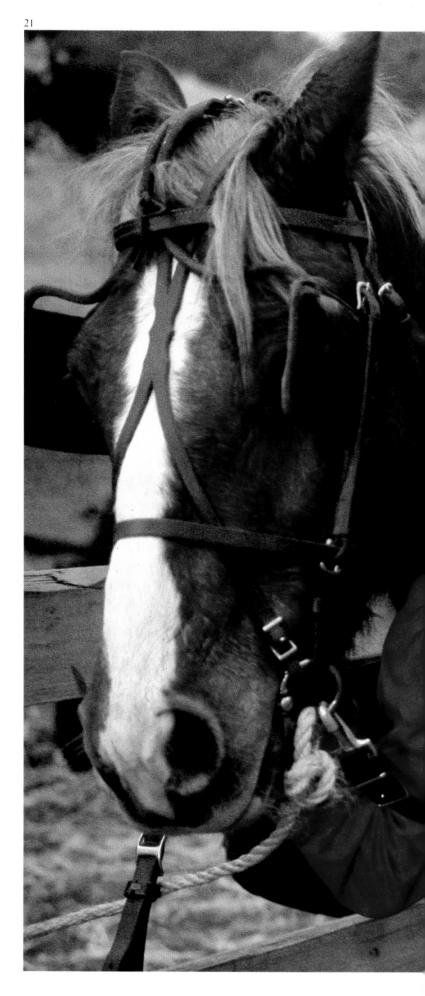

am good and can handle it. After I worked a few jobs, they started coming more frequently.

Getting the job is only the beginning of the battle. Once I arrive on the set, I have no idea what I'm going to be asked to do. You want to get the job done as safely as possible and at the same time make it look spectacular. I have worked many times on *Little House on the Prairie*. I talked to people connected with the show for nearly a year trying to get hired. It was like talking to a wall. I was finally hired because they had to double a small boy driving a team of horses and riding bareback. The job ran very smoothly. They were pleased enough with my work to have me double Hersha Parady while I was there.

Since then, I have become a regular double for Melissa Gilbert and have also doubled Steve Tracey in the show. Unfortunately, the jobs don't always run smoothly. Working with horses is very unpredictable. Generally, the stunt man has never seen the horse he is going to work with, and horses are like people—they're all different.

In one episode of *Little House on the Prairie* I doubled Melissa driving a buggy. The horse was supposed to be unbroken, and Half-Pint trains him. They wanted the horse to rear up and jump around and be able to act calm later in the script. They trained him to rear and act crazy if you picked up the reins and put pressure on his mouth. If you gave him his head, he was fine.

In the scenes where I drove him at a gallop or a trot, he was fine. The scene that should have been the hardest went perfectly. I had to start with him rearing and running away, then bring him down to a trot, turn him and walk right into the camera. The following morning I tried to do what should have been the easiest shot of the show. It was a near disaster. I'm just walking slowly up the road having a conversation with the doctor (doubled by Carl Pitti). I'm in my buggy; he's walking alongside of his. The director

Veteran stunt man Carl Pitti (23) instructs Cindy for a runaway carriage stunt. The director maps out the action to wranglers, technicians and stunt men (24).

had specified he wanted us walking. Well, my horse didn't want to walk, and when I tried to check him back, he started to rear and jump around. I ruined the take. I was yelled at and thoroughly embarrassed.

The camera starts to roll (25), and Cindy drives the carriage toward it (26, 27 & 28). This scene was repeated three times.

The horse I fall in these pictures belongs to Carl and his daughter, Karla. Her name is Flozac. Flozac is an exceptional animal. She is now twenty years old, and Karla showed her for years as a jumper. Most horses in the business are trained to do one thing and not much more, but Flozac does it all. Karla and I have jumped her, fallen her, done transfers, bulldogs and swingups on her.

29

30

Most falling horses are hard to make fall. Basically you cue a falling horse by grabbing the right rein and pulling its head around while its front legs are reaching for the next stride. Most horses can be fallen about twice. After that they'll cheat you and won't want to fall. Flozac is a different story. The day we shot the pictures, I fell her twenty-five times in a row, and she never cheated me once.

My husband, Jeff Ramsey, also works as a stunt man. He and I had the opportunity of working together in a Universal film for television called *Masada*. The scene we worked in was the one in which the Romans are conquering the Jews. We worked at night on the backlot at Universal Studios. Jeff was a Roman soldier on horseback, I was a Jewish peasant woman on foot. All the buildings around us were on fire, and horses and extras were running frantically through the streets. I came running down the street screaming, with Jeff's horse on my heels. He backed me into a wall. I attempted to fight back, but he grabbed me by the hair. He then took off galloping and dragged me through the street.

On the set of Charlie Chan and the Curse of the Dragon Lady, *the horse Cindy will ride has a blaze painted on its face (29) to double for the horse to be used later by actress Michelle Pfeiffer. Michelle watches while Cindy is made up as her double (30). Cindy and actor Richard Hatch listen to instructions from the director (31).*

31

This was a difficult stunt. The special-effects man rigged me in a harness (under my costume). Attached to the harness was a cable that went through the braid in my wig. That way, when Jeff grabbed the braid it didn't rip the wig, and my hair, off.

Some jobs look very easy, but they are really very dangerous. I doubled the actress Audrey Landers in the film *Underground Aces*. We filmed at the Airport Marriott Hotel in Los Angeles. In this particular scene the hotel catches fire during Miss Landers' wedding. Everybody runs out of the hotel, where there is an underground horseshoe driveway. The driveway is on a steep bank and the

(32) A trainer practices the double's rear. Cindy is given a leg up (33), listens to last-minute instructions (34-35), and rides off (36) to wait for the call.

pavement as slick as ice. At the same time the screaming guests are running up, police cars and fire engines are driving down, sirens going, lining the drive with lights. At this time the Sheikh in his flowing robes comes galloping down the driveway on horseback.

The first take, the horse lost his footing and fell (luckily the stunt man was not hurt). He rode in again, picked me up (I rode sidesaddle in front of him), and we galloped out. If it hadn't been for the slick pavement, it would have been an extremely easy job, but with the fire engines

parked in the driveway, it only left us a few feet's width to work in. If we had fallen, there would have been nowhere for us to go. It worked out fine.

Being young and still new in the business, I feel that I'm on probation, so I don't want to make any mistakes. I never accept a job unless I feel qualified for it. Once I misjudged, and because of my inexperience it was one of the

On cue she rides the horse toward the camera and rears it (37) as Richard Hatch runs toward her. The fall and continuing action are seen in (38-45).

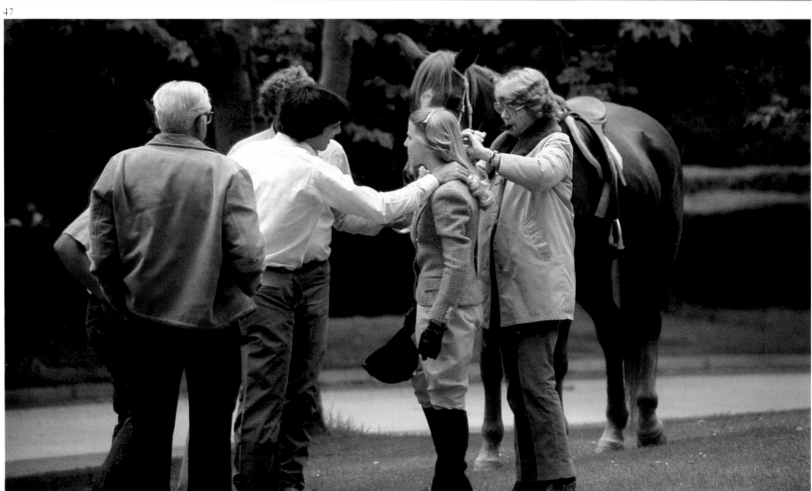

worst days of my life. I doubled Michelle Pfeiffer in the film *Charlie Chan and the Curse of the Dragon Lady.* We were shooting at the Doheny Estate in Beverly Hills. My job was to ride the horse, English-style, at a canter down a hill and into camera. At this point Richard Hatch jumps out and throws his arms in the air, frightening the horse. I then cue the horse to rear up and I fall off. This horse's cue was to squeeze him with my legs and pick him up with my hands.

I have small hands, and the reins were wide, and they gave me a bouquet of flowers and a riding crop to carry. I had a hard time just getting my fingers around the reins.

When I just reared the horse without falling, I would get a nice high rise from him. Because of my inexperience, I didn't yet have the timing for the rear and the fall, and so frequently I couldn't get him to rear up as high as we wanted. Another obstacle was not being able to use a step. In most falls you put a step on your saddle, higher than your stirrup. When it's time to fall, you use your foot to push off the step and it helps you make the fall, but because of the camera angle on *Charlie Chan,* I couldn't use it. That made my fall a little delayed.

In stunt work you always have to hit a mark. So, in a scene like this I have to ride into a certain spot to do the rear, and then fall and land in a precise place for the camera. Well, after we did this a few times, the horse didn't want to go into his mark anymore. He knew the actor was going to jump out. I hit the ground so many times that day, just thinking of it makes me feel sick. Fortunately, of all the jobs I've done, this was the only one that was really disastrous.

There is a lot of competition and a lot of jealousy in the motion-picture industry. People don't say much if you do something well, but if you make a mistake, the news is usually exaggerated and spread all over town. All I can do is try my hardest to do a good job, because when I do a really good job, the feeling is such a high that it makes it all worthwhile.

After the first take, Cindy is congratulated (46) and briefed (47) for a repeat of the stunt. The take over, Cindy and Michelle walk to the wardrobe trailer to change (48). Later Cindy watches Michelle being made up (49) and being filmed falling from a standing horse (50).

MARÍA ELENA CASTAÑEDA
mexico

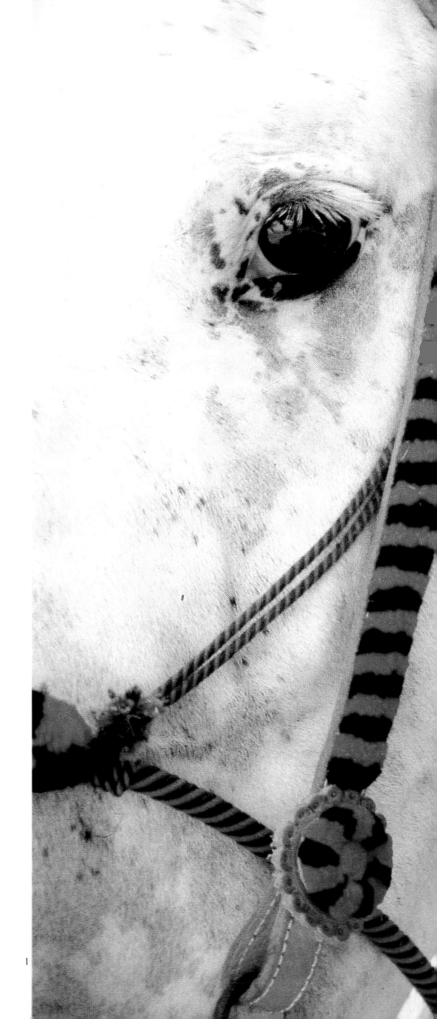

*S*ome years ago in Seville I remember going to a bullfight at the end of which a drill team of Mexican horsewomen, called escaramuzas, performed. It was one of the most colorful and exciting demonstrations of horsemanship I have seen. Those Mexican girls, all with broad-brimmed hats, full skirts and petticoats, and riding sidesaddle, looked like a handful of flowers thrown to the wind, swirling across the sand of the Maestranza bullring to captivate the Spanish crowd completely. It was then that I decided to one day photograph escaramuzas in action.

Fifteen years later, when this book was started, a Mexican girl and a troupe of escaramuzas were a priority. I had decided to photograph the escaramuzas in Mexico City, where friends had offered to make arrangements for me. But in the end it was in Tijuana that I found what I was looking for—the Escaramuza Charra of Tijuana.

Unfortunately, the Winter and Spring of 1980 were the wettest Baja California had seen in years. Day after day I was rained out, and when the sun did shine, María Elena Castañeda, the queen of the Escaramuza Charra of Tijuana, was ill and I began to doubt if I would ever photograph her. Finally, though, came a weekend when the rain stopped, and María Elena was able to come to Tijuana.

I spent wonderful days with the girls of the Misión del Sol. There were afternoon charriadas, a Mexican rodeo, in which María Elena and the troupe performed, and lunches of carne asada and tortillas. Once I suggested that we take María Elena and her horse, Paloma, to a nearby beach for some additional shots. Within minutes a picnic was organized, and soon I was sitting high on a cliff while María Elena rode her white mare through the surf of the Pacific below.

(1) Queen of the Escaramuza Charra of Tijuana, María Elena Castañeda, with her mare, Paloma.

My name is María Elena Castañeda Silva, and I was born in Tijuana, Baja California. I am sixteen years old and attend high school, and I hope soon to study law at the university. Horses are my sport, my passion and my life. For five years I have been a member of the Escaramuza Charra of Tijuana, which has meant a great deal of hard work, effort and dedication, and many difficulties.

I don't think I will ever forget the first time I took part in a training practice. A school friend who already belonged to the group invited me along, and after much pleading I was allowed to go. I found some pretty pants, a fashionable blouse and some very elegant boots, and made myself as smart as I could. Finally, the great day

came, and all the way there it seemed to me that my mother was driving slower than ever, I was so impatient to arrive. My mother had always maintained that the escaramuza was very dangerous, and I argued that it wasn't so bad and that I would be very careful.

The group practicing was the children's escaramuza. They were all about my age and there was even a little girl of four, who was very good; I think it was seeing her that decided my mother to let me join the group. That was the first, good impression, but everything wasn't so pleasant that day. Accidents don't always happen, but this day one of the girls was doing a maneuver on her horse when it tripped and they both crashed to the ground. Everyone

3

4

5

nearby ran to help her, but I saw only my mother's face and thought, 'that is the end of that.' When the training finished, the instructress invited me to come down from the stand, and I was introduced to the girls I didn't know. They all greeted me warmly and explained how to work the reins and how I should sit in the special saddle, which I had never seen before. They gave me the quietest horse in the stable, an old sorrel Quarter-horse mare called La Gringa.

María Elena waits with the others for a workout to begin (2). One of the most precise escaramuza exercises is the Abanico, or Fan (3–6).

6

My enthusiasm grew greater every moment, and I thought my heart would burst through the silk shirt that I had chosen so carefully. Everything was perfect; I felt I had gained the world that day—except that I sensed the rejection of the other girls. I hadn't expected them all to accept me straightaway, but what was my mistake? I wanted to be part of the group. When I was leaving, the instructress said to me, "Next time you come, wear Levis and boots with low heels, and try not to grumble so much about getting your face dirty." I realized what was wrong—everyone else wore hard-wearing pants, a plain blouse and boots made for spurs, and no one worried about getting dirty. I learned many things that day that will be useful to me all my life.

I should tell you that by the second practice, I had mended my ways and was accepted by the girls, and since then we have been a truly friendly, cooperative group.

I should explain, too, that the escaramuza charra is a group of Mexican women who perform very dangerous exercises and movements on horseback, displaying great skill, precision and bravery. Most of the exercises are done in the ring at varying speeds, which makes them resemble a ballet on horseback.

María Elena talks with girl friends and charro singer Gualo Silva (8) before the crowning ceremony (9).

There are no words to describe clearly the impression made on people who see an escaramuza group perform for the first time. You can see reflected in their faces fright, joy and apprehension, and I have sometimes seen people with tears of emotion in their eyes after watching a small girl, mounted on a spirited horse, with no other desire than to show her fidelity to the Mexican traditions that her parents have taught her from the cradle.

If I describe my first horse to you, you will think it was the most beautiful horse in the world, so I'll only say that it was a sorrel Arab that had belonged to one of the escaramuzas, and that she had had to sell when she moved away. My horse had many good qualities: he was gentle, he performed the movements of the escaramuza very well and he was very quick. But above all I liked him very much, and that made up for any defects. He was called Bonito. I only had him for two years, when he hurt a tendon and it couldn't be cured, and the vet said he should be put down. To comfort me my father said we would take

María Elena and escaramuza directors Rosalinda Soler de Gutiérrez and Guadalupe Soler de Solís, in the marketplace after the parade (10). María Elena is serenaded by a group of mariachis before the Mexican rodeo or charriada (11). Paloma saddled (12) for the charriada.

12

him to a ranch where he could live without working, and that is what we did. It is a tragedy for anyone to lose their horse, and I was only fourteen and he was my first. My only consolation was that he didn't have to die, but could go on living even though away from me.

Now I was without a horse and had to look for a new one. I was more knowledgeable now, and I wanted a stronger and showier horse on which I could demonstrate all I had learned. I found Paloma, a beautiful Appaloosa mare that belonged to one of the charros, but for all my pleading he wouldn't sell her to me. However, at last, because of some financial problems he had, he was forced to give in and Paloma became mine. Her name wasn't really Paloma before I bought her, but I wanted her so badly that I had even given her a new name.

As for horses in general, each member of the group buys the animal that suits her best, but the ideal horse for the escaramuza is tall and strong, because the work is very tiring. It should not be hard-mouthed, although of course the girls in the escaramuza are capable of riding any horse. Nor is it possible to talk of the beauty of the horses that make up our group, for each girl believes her horse to be the most beautiful in the world, and it is a tragedy if any horse is injured, so I will just say that our parents try to buy us the very best horses.

The equipment consists of a sidesaddle like those once used by Spanish women in colonial times. It consists of a wooden frame covered in leather, which makes the seat very comfortable. The rider uses only the left stirrup, hooking her right leg over the saddle horn; both her legs are then on the left. As well as the sidesaddle there is a saddle cloth, a serape, a martingale and a special bridle. All these are made in Mexico in the charra tradition.

Without a doubt the charra costume is sumptuous and varied; it ranges from a simple cotton gown to a charra suit embroidered in silver and gold. I will describe the costume worn when taking part in a competition in the ring. It consists of a very full skirt and a high-necked blouse with either long or short sleeves. These clothes should be as brightly and contrastingly colored as possible, to give gaiety and life to the ring. Under the skirt is a shorter petticoat and tight pants that are tucked into boots. The boots come to just below the knees and are called Jalisco boots. A spur is worn on the left boot. Complementing this outfit is a broad-brimmed hat, kept on by a leather thong under the chin.

For those of you who have never seen an escaramuza charra, I will try to describe some of the maneuvers we perform.

The Flower: In this exercise the riders, in two groups of four, take up a fan-shaped formation. At the signal the rear group weaves its horses through the line in front of them and then, having ridden in a circle around the ring (like the hand of a clock), takes up position in line at the front. The original front line, now at the rear, repeats the movement.

The Braid: The braid has always been and always will be a characteristic of the Mexican woman from the Aztec and

María Elena followed by escaramuzas and charros, leads the parade into the ring (13). Once the group has crossed the ring, individual charros show off their horsemanship (14 & 15).

16

colonial times to the present day; any representation of a Mexican woman without braids is inconceivable.

The difficulty of this movement lies in the narrowness of the space between each horse and the need to coordinate the horses' speeds, since when riding in a circle, the horse at the center only trots while the one at the edge of the ring must gallop to maintain a straight line.

And as the braid is so Mexican, we do an exercise in the ring which resembles the plaiting of a braid of hair. Horses and riders form groups to represent strands of hair, and in a very graceful movement weave themselves into one line.

Having changed into her escaramuza costume, María Elena gallops Paloma across the ring to pull the mare up short in the Rayo, or Skid exercise (16-19).

17

18

Two long files are formed, the horses on the left passing to the right and vice versa, until just the one file remains to gallop out of the ring.

The Fan: The fan has always been used by very feminine women, more for flirting than to keep cool, and the escaramuza has called one of its numbers, which requires daring, skill, speed and control—and smiles on the faces of its performers—the Fan.

The exercise consists of riding horses around the ring in a line like the large hand of a clock—the rider at the center only trots, while those toward the outside ride successively faster so as to maintain a straight line. The whole impression is of an opening fan.

The French Knot: As every woman knows, a French knot is an attractive arrangement of hair worn at the back of the head. The Escaramuza Charra of Tijuana has named one of its movements the Moño, or Knot, because it forms loops resembling a knot of hair.

At a given moment all the odd-numbered girls in the charra begin to form a small circle, while all the even-numbered ones ride around the edge of the ring until the inner circle is completely formed. At this point they begin to weave their horses through the smaller circle and out the other side to make their own small circle, through which the odd-numbered girls weave in their turn, thus forming loops like a knot of hair.

Looking like moving blossoms on the sand, María Elena and the escaramuzas perform the Moño, or French Knot, in which they ride in figure eights, cutting in and out of one another (20-25).

Crossings of Death: Why this name, you will ask, and where is the femininity she was talking about? Really, it is very difficult for me to explain on paper just what the exercises of the escaramuzas are like. Written words are too cold to describe the emotions we feel—those moments must be experienced to be understood. I can only say that this exercise is well-named, because it is very

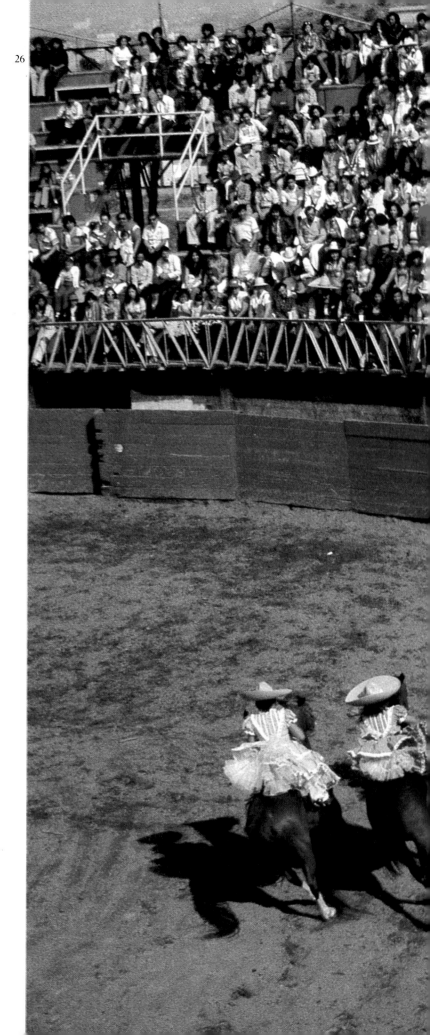

(26) The escaramuzas gallop round the ring in the Fan. María and a friend race toward center ring to perform a double Skid, each rider reflecting the movements of the other (27-30).

dangerous, and more than once I have seen horses crash head on, breaking their legs, and girls often have serious falls.

It is performed by making two circles, and at a gallop the girls of each circle pass into the other circle, thus forming a figure eight, or a cross, on the ground. At the moment of crossing, the horse's head must be as close as possible to the tail of the one that crosses in front of it, and this is when the rider feels a surge of joy, to see how her horse doesn't falter but passes at exactly the right moment, to the wild applause of the crowd.

The Skid: This number can be done individually, which I think is most satisfying for the performer, or in pairs, which makes it more difficult.

It is performed by galloping down the center of the entrance to the ring and out across the sand, pulling up the horse so suddenly that it skids on its haunches to the center of the ring.

This is a very complex exercise, and there are many details to be taken into account: The horse should not resist the initial rush into the ring; it must be urged to gallop faster; it must stop in the center of the ring; the skid marks should be of a certain length and made only with the hind legs; the horse's mouth should remain shut when it is being pulled up; it should not buck or rear; and many more things too numerous to list.

The Rake: The charra divides into two groups, which form lines, then wheel and face each other across the ring. They gallop toward each other, one line passing through the other near the center of the ring, and continue to the other side, where they wheel and repeat the movement.

Of all the maneuvers, the Fan is the crowd's favorite. María Elena in two of the costumes that she uses for performances (31 & 32).

It has been an emotional experience for me to write these lines for you, who live in places very different from my own country, with distinct customs and habits, but who have something very beautiful in common—the love of horses. Horses throughout history have been close to man and have always had a special place in his heart. And to all of you who love horses I send a most sincere invitation to visit Mexico and especially a charra fiesta, so that what I have been unable to explain clearly you may experience for yourselves.

At my school I recently entered a poetry competition, and my inspiration was Paloma, my mare.

MI YEGUA

Es mi yegua la paloma
De belleza sin igual
Cuando monto yo en su lomo
Necesito sofrenar
Estas ansias de mi alma
Que me dicen ¡corre más!
Es su andar de tal belleza
Que parece coquetear
Y el manchado de sus ancas
Lo parece reafirmar.

(33 & 34) María Elena riding Paloma through the Pacific surf not far from Misión del Sol.

DEBI JENSEN
usa

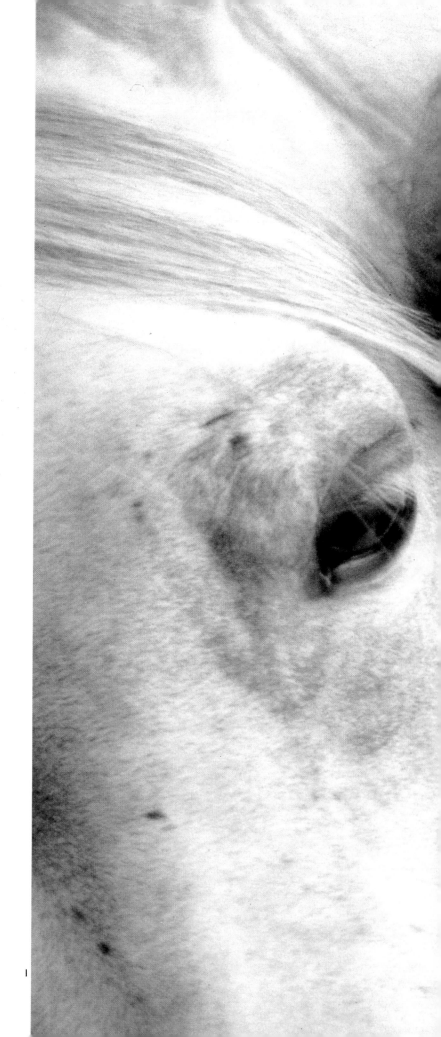

*I*t was a photograph in a horse magazine of a girl riding an almost-white Arab stallion through a forest, without saddle or bridle, that led me to Oregon and Debi Jensen. The editor of the magazine put me in touch with Betty Notley, the owner of the stallion, Wazir, and the mother of the girl in the picture.

I met Betty at the winter Arab show in Scottsdale, Arizona, and it was arranged for me to visit Raintree Egyptian Stud, Betty's farm in Oregon. A month later, just as I was setting off for Oregon, Betty rang me up to say that her daughter, Rainy, was ill and would be unable to ride for the photographs. Being so close to Oregon and knowing that I would be unable to return before leaving for Europe, I asked Betty if it was all right if I came anyway, and she agreed.

At Raintree I met Betty's trainer, Debi Jensen, and found an ideal subject. Trainer, stud manager, horse-show judge and competitor, it would be difficult to find a young woman as talented, good-looking and hard-working as Debi. She also has a marvelous sense of humor, which made working with her and Wazir one of the most enjoyable moments of this book.

It particularly impressed me that Debi, in spite of being divorced and having a young daughter to bring up, had continued her career with horses. I hope that her story will serve as an inspiration to other young women. Watching Debi work on the farm and in the show ring was fascinating, but trailing after her as she rode Wazir bareback and bridleless, using only a slim piece of cord around his neck to guide his wild gallops, made me feel almost as though I were witness to some medieval fairy tale brought to life.

I've never become deeply involved in astrology, so I can't be sure, but maybe being born a Sagittarian has something to do with my life revolving around horses.

It surprises many people that a girl raised in the city should end up with a vocation such as mine. My mother

(1) Judge, trainer and stud manager of Arabian horses Debi Jensen, with Egyptian-bred stallion Wazir.

152

spent nineteen years thinking I'd outgrow horses. Surely when I entered high school and started dating boys, I'd develop new interests. But I fooled her! I dated all right, but most of my boyfriends had horses too! Apart from my sister, Cindi, who's always had a mild case of horse fever herself, I've been the only horse nut in the family. This has been a real handicap at times, because only another horse nut understands the worth of these costly animals and all the paraphernalia that goes along with them.

It took lots of begging and promises to convince my mother to buy the first horse. And, thinking back, I'm sure that the embarrassment she must have felt watching us gallop all over the neighborhood on dust mops and brooms, pretending they were horses, must have been the clincher. So, at six years old I was in for the experience of a lifetime: my first horse. We named him Gypsy King, after a beautiful racehorse. He was a golden palomino with a long silky mane and tail. Tall and flashy, it was easy to see why his previous owner had ridden him in parades.

Now, twenty-one years later, I look back at the pictures of King and realize we were a little barn blind. He wasn't

Debi talks to six young trainees who work on the ranch (2). The trainees with Wazir (3). A mare is brought in for breeding (4).

3

actually a golden palomino, he was more of a faded yellow; his mane wasn't exactly long and silky, it was kind of bushy and gray. His flashy way of moving was anything but desirable by my standards today. But King was a real live horse and, most important, he was *my* horse. Even if I could have seen all his faults then, I wouldn't have loved him less.

King was the beginning of a career that led from 4-H, through show jumping and rodeo queening, to training and showing Arab horses professionally, until I was twenty, when I got married. My husband was in the cattle business and we were always on the move. We moved to Colorado, Oklahoma, Texas, Missouri, back to Colorado and Oklahoma, always to different cities. When we were in Texas, I worked cattle in an auction yard; in Missouri I

The Raintree breeding program is an important part of Debi's work. (5, 6 & 7) Debi and Betty Notley mate Wazir to one of the ranch's mares.

found myself teaching at a riding school; and in Colorado, where my daughter, Sunny, was born, I spent eight months in charge of the breaking and pretrack training of two-year-old Quarter-horse colts for a racing trainer. And then we moved to Tulsa, Oklahoma.

When we arrived it was midsummer, and it was so hot and humid we thought we'd melt. I spent a great deal of time at home inside with the air conditioning and had time to miss my career with the horses. It was not practical to try to establish myself as a trainer, moving as we did, but I needed to be involved again. Finally, it occurred to me that since I had always been interested in judging, it was something that I could do from anywhere. Big shows never use local judges (to avoid any favoritism), so you judge out of town.

My first step was to gather some information. I sent off a few letters and made phone calls, but things really started when a very respected judge, Don Burt, was in Tulsa judging a show. He told me about the "learner judge" system and agreed to let me tag along with him to some shows.

Getting the arrangements made for the first show was difficult. I made a serious error as far as the show manager was concerned. I first consulted the American Horse Show Association, and then the local show association. Little did I know that I had to do just the opposite. It took a lot of talking and apologies to smooth ruffled feathers and get things arranged.

There were two other judges working the show with Don Burt, as is often the case in larger shows. At first, I thought that meant three times the pressure and they'd all be watching me with critical eyes, but I soon found out I was wrong. These three, kind, talented men spent the entire weekend helping, teaching and teasing me. I can't

When Wazir has been unloaded at the showgrounds, Debi lunges him (8) and then practices for the halter class (9).

remember when I had more fun. I asked Don if he always had this much fun at the shows, and his remark made a great impression on me: "If it ever stops being this much fun, I'll quit doing it." We worked very, very hard during the show, especially when the classes were in the ring, but between sessions there was a lot of light conversation and a few good jokes. This really helped all of us to stay relaxed during what could have been a stressful job. Not all judges are like this, but I learned from these three how to enjoy the job.

I knew if being a learner judge at one show was good, being a learner judge at ten would be even better. So I did more. I asked Don to recommend other judges I could work with who would have similar judging opinions to his. It was important for me to learn from the very best.

Don recommended a Canadian named Peter Cameron. When I looked him up in the rule book, I saw he was the highest-rated judge in the business. It was going to be a hard move. I had become so fond of Don and felt comfortable working with him. Surely Mr. Cameron had to be a stuffed shirt. When we first met at the airport, that was just the impression I got. I remember thinking, 'Thanks a lot, Don, sticking me with this guy for three days.' My first impressions of people are usually correct, but this time I couldn't have been more wrong. As we got to know each other we became very good friends, and he shared judging knowledge and techniques that you can't find in any book, special things you can only explain in person.

At Arabian shows, Debi often competes in Arabian costume (10), Park (11 & 12), sidesaddle (13), and western classes (14).

13

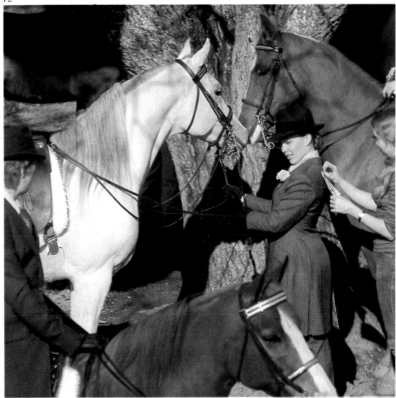

I knew it would take a lot of time before I could be kept busy enough judging to please myself, so I took a job with an aircraft dealer as a contract liaison. This was a very exciting, challenging position, but every time I passed a horse trailer on the way to work, it got harder and harder to go inside the office.

Debi working Wazir in the four mounted classes (15-18) and in the halter class (19). Debi and Wazir have been awarded many trophies and ribbons (20).

A letter from Pat Mauck, an old friend and a highly successful trainer, made me realize how much I missed the horse business. We exchanged some plans over the phone, and soon my husband and I made a move for *my* career. I couldn't have been happier. Finally, I was back in Oregon and close to my family and old friends, and back at work training. I had a lot of catching up to do. Pat had really progressed and had some new techniques. She spent a lot of time teaching me improved methods that have proved highly successful and have been helpful to me ever since.

At that time Pat had several special horses, but one that stood out was a beautiful white-gray stallion named Gdansk. Pat had made this horse a real celebrity after other trainers said he was untrainable. Under Pat's direction Gdansk became so popular that we quickly outgrew the facility we were using. At times we had over eighty horses, and, unfortunately, this stable offered no pastures or paddocks. Every horse had to be kept in its stall until we took it into the arena for exercise periods. This was not satisfactory for the horses or us. Pat found a ranch in Redmond, Oregon, which was large enough to allow the horses to be kept outside, and we then moved ourselves and about fifty horses to the new location.

Seven years had passed since I had been as actively involved in training and showing as Pat and I were then. On top of this, and ending up with nearly two hundred horses on the new ranch during breeding season, I had started a program of my own called Twin Fir Amateur Owners, giving lessons to more accomplished riders who wished to train and show their own horses instead of having a trainer do all the work. This program became so popular that it soon had me working seven days a week and about ten hours a day. This didn't leave much time for my daughter or husband, so something had to give. Pat and I discussed this and decided it could be a good move for me to go on with the Amateur Owners Program and to drop the job with her.

Betty Notley and Debi watch Wazir and three of the ranch's other stallions on the hot walker (21). Debi judging young Arabian horses (22).

Just as this was happening, my husband and I decided to get divorced. We had not been getting along for some time now and it seemed to be the only solution. With all this happening, the final blow occurred when a mare I was working fell and I broke my leg. This meant spending the entire show season on the sidelines.

My husband had gone to Colorado and I could hardly get around, so my daughter and I moved in with my parents. We were lucky to have them there to help us through this rough period. Just when my cast was taken off, I received a phone call. The enthusiastic voice belonged to Betty Notley of Raintree Egyptian Stud in Newberg, Oregon, about forty miles from my parents'

It is a spectacular sight to see Debi riding Wazir without bridle or saddle through the Oregon forest, using only her legs and a light cord to guide him (23). Even when Wazir is approached by mares in season (24), he remains loyal to his rider, pausing only to signal to them with his head and his eyes (25).

home. Betty explained that she needed a new manager-trainer and had heard I might be available. At first, I wasn't too interested. I still had a limp and didn't know how long it would be before my leg would permit me to train again. Betty convinced me that I should see the facility and talk to her. As soon as I drove into the ranch with its long drive lined with trees and its flags in the ranch colors, its beautiful white barns and newly finished arena, I was impressed, but Betty herself was a real selling point. She was friendly and eager to go to the top. We seemed to have so much in common that we felt we would be a great team.

The first few weeks at Raintree were hectic, to say the least. I was so busy trying to learn all about the operation and the fifty or so head of horses on the ranch that I had time for nothing else. The healing leg was very painful for the first couple of months. Finally, it started to get better, and the limp has now disappeared.

As I became better acquainted with Egyptian-bred Arabians, I soon gained a deep respect for these people-oriented horses. Never have I worked with such willing animals; many of the young ones that we start riding shortly after their third birthday accept the saddle and rider without question. Their instinct to serve man is very strong.

The finest example of an Egyptian-bred Arabian, in my opinion, is Ansata El Wazir. Never before have I worked with a stallion that can be communicated with so easily and trusted so much. Wazir possesses an almost human personality, and a very likable one at that! It is easy to see why he draws people to him. People who never particularly liked horses stop and want to touch Wazir. Artists come to paint and photograph him.

It is a common practice to keep stallions away from the other horses on a farm. This is to protect the horses from their instinct to fight; in the wild a stallion will fight off other males in order to keep all the mares to himself. It is

(26-34) Debi not only demonstrates her ability and sensitivity as a horsewoman but also Wazir's nobility.

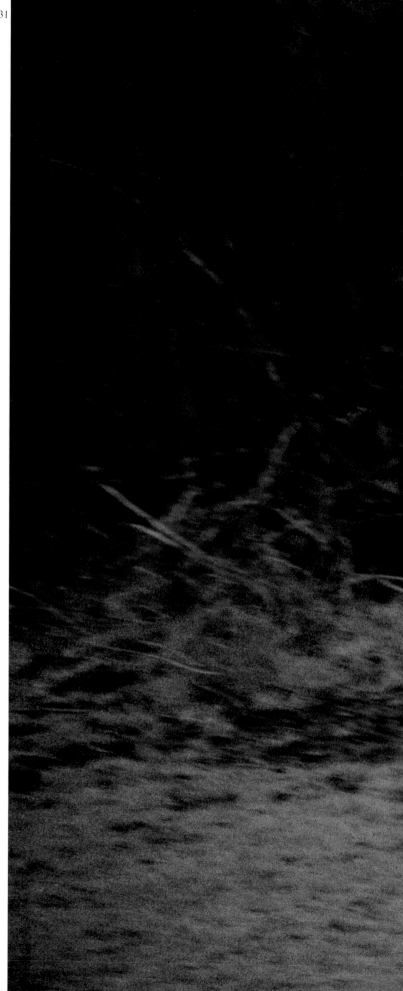

highly unusual to ride any stallion without a saddle or bridle for control, let alone among loose mares and foals. But Wazir seems to take all this in stride, he seems to know there is no need to try to ditch his rider and to run off with the mares. He has all the mares he could ever want brought right to his barn each day of the breeding season.

Another unusual quirk of Wazir's personality is his emotional involvement with the mares he covers each year. Out of the many that are brought to him, one mare we call Donna remains his true and first love. From anywhere, at anytime, when Wazir sees his beloved Donna, he will call her and watch her for hours. Many of the other mares seem to bore him; and we sometimes have to bring Donna to lift his spirits when he isn't in the mood for another female. It's also interesting to note that Donna is the most gentle of all the mares. Maybe they care for each other because they are so much alike.

From the descriptions of Wazir so far it would be easy to conclude that he is just a quiet, lazy old horse, but this couldn't be farther from the truth. When people come to visit, we turn him loose in the arena and he curls his tail over his back and snorts and struts like a really hot-blooded stallion. Then, after a couple of minutes of this, we mount him, or even let many first-time riders climb on his back, and he carefully carries them around the ring.

I am twenty-eight now and I feel very lucky to be able to earn my living doing something I love. There are many times when there is too much work and I get tense and unhappy, but even with this to deal with, I will never leave the horse world. In my present position I am head trainer and manager for Raintree Egyptian Stud. Here we not only breed, sell and train, we assist owners in their own breeding programs, and instructions (or lessons) are available for those who want them. We house over ninety head of horses in the busy spring months when we are breeding and foaling the mares. Throughout the winter we usually care for approximately fifty head.

My job combines a variety of duties, from the actual breeding and training of the horses to the sales and business relations. I have learned that even though I have a vocation with horses, I am still very much in the people business, as it is the public's high opinion and approval that we strive for in the breeding and training of our animals. As time goes by, I hope to accomplish even more and produce many champions through my insight as a breeding advisor and my efforts as a trainer. However, there will be a time when I will not want to bear the physical stress that I take now in training, and then I will spend more time judging, managing and teaching others to communicate with this truly remarkable animal, the horse.

INGE
SCHULZE
germany

*W*et weather plagued this book not only in America and Mexico but also in Europe. The Summer of 1980 had been Europe's wettest in years. But by the end of July it had stopped raining, and I flew to Düsseldorf to photograph Inge Schulze, twice Junior Dressage Champion of Europe.

My spirits sank as we approached Düsseldorf Airport and the plane was suddenly swirled in gray clouds and rain. The next day, however, as I drove to the Essen home of Inge's uncle, the trainer Fritz Templemann, the sun was shining. And if the day was bright, so were my spirits when I was introduced to Inge, a girl with beautiful eyes and a radiant smile.

Fritz Templemann has such a special way about him that his success as a trainer both of horses and young riders is not surprising. And he has a charming wife who helped me a great deal—as did Inge's brother, Bernard, and their friend, Heinrich.

I had hoped to photograph Inge out of the ring with its distracting white fences. At first, this seemed impossible, but after working for a day, she agreed to take one of her horses to a nearby field. It was there that I wanted to photograph various dressage movements and especially the extended trot.

As I write this, the film of Inge has not yet been developed. I can only hope that the field was as green as it is in my memory, and that the camera was able to capture the fluidness and grace of Inge and her horse against it.

People frequently confuse dressage with breaking in, or imagine it to be somewhat artificial. This is not the case. The classical art of riding is based strictly on the laws of nature and cannot in any way be compared with trick riding or circus riding. Basically dressage is only a further development of the horse's natural gait, which the trainer strives to maintain in its essential purity and beauty. The

(1) Inge Schulze, twice European Junior Dressage Champion, and her horse, Don Benito.

idea is to increase the horse's pace in walking, trotting and galloping, and to refine and perfect it through a series of exercises. Therefore, a harmony must be developed between horse and rider. It is this harmony that is the final result aimed for in all dressage.

The love of horses and riding is very strong in my family. My father was in the mounted police and my grandfather was also a keen horseman. The other members of my family are all connected with riding in one way or another. What else could I be but a rider? Even before I could walk properly I spent all my time at the nearest stables, and more often than not on the back of a horse. When I was about three years old, I began to learn

Inge's uncle, the trainer, Fritz Templemann, talks to her at his stable near Essen (2). Inge in the tackroom (3) and leading a horse to the stable (4).

vaulting and worked at it so hard that, thanks to my height, I was soon able to vault onto the horse's back un-aided. Even then it seemed easier to mount by using the stirrups—and so my career as a rider began.

In my hand-me-down breeches I became in time the most industrious "dry rider" at our stables. My job was to take the horses that had been worked to a sweat and ride them, at a walk with slack reins, until they were dry. My first attempts at trotting and galloping were made on the sly, and I quickly developed a routine so that the dry-ing of the horses seemed to take longer and longer every day. About that time I was given the opportunity, thanks to my father, to learn the basics of riding without having to be secretive about it.

Three of the horses used by Inge in competitions—Pascal, Paquito and Don Benito (5 & 6). Inge with Pascal (7).

Riding Pascal, Inge executes the Piaffe (8-10).

My big chance came when my uncle, Fritz Templemann, an internationally known trainer of riders and horses who I thought would never notice me, offered me a place in his young riders' group. He also gave me a horse. These riding lessons are some of my most wonderful memories. Thanks to the others in the group and to my uncle's originality, we had lots of fun. We could hardly stop laughing at some of his more outrageous criticisms of our poor riding. Not that there was any lack

(12-14) Inge braids Don Benito's mane. In (15-20) Inge and Pascal perform the Passage.

16

15

18

17

20

19

of proper seriousness. On the contrary, my uncle taught with concentration and was a strict disciplinarian; punctuality, well-groomed horses and highly polished boots were of the utmost importance. To contradict was absolutely forbidden. For not paying attention we would have to practice mounting and dismounting until we were perfect, or spend hours leading the horse by hand until we had it just right. However, we accepted this strictness without rancor, and it was justified by our rapid advancement.

From this point on, my riding was more steady but even at that stage it was clear that it required sacrifices on my part. Often I would have to get up at five in the morning to go riding. As far as I can remember, I spent a year under my uncle's supervision, riding the horses until they were dry and, later, saddling and unsaddling them. Riding was a privilege that had to be earned, and the fact that I was related to my teacher was not allowed to help. But even if it was hard to be forced to watch the others ride, I accepted it and today I am thankful for this time of learning.

In my second year I was allowed to untie the horses and warm them up, something that, having seen it done so often, I could do—at least in theory. And then, by chance, I was able to add to my training under optimal conditions. Uncle Fritz had an operation and was unable to ride for some time. And so my wish came true, I was allowed to ride one of his horses. Every morning I was driven from school to the stables; I rode three of his horses and had lessons at the same time. It was strenuous, but I learned a lot—nothing escaped the trained eye of Uncle Fritz.

Most likely it was at this stage that the decision was taken to make a rider out of me. I threw myself into it

One of the most beautiful of dressage movements is the extended trot. The horse seems literally to glide across the field (21-25).

26   27   28

29   30   31

34   33   32

35   36   37

body and soul, I was hooked on dressage. Soon I was putting horses that were boarded at my uncle's for training through their paces, and after a while, I did the same with his own horses. Whenever one of these horses was sold, I had to get used to a new one. It was not easy for me, especially if I had loved the horse.

The real moment of decision came six years ago, when Uncle Fritz bought me a black horse called Don Benito. Don Benito was distinguished by unusual talent, and I was only too happy to be involved in his training from the beginning. To this horse, and to Uncle Fritz, I owe

everything that I have so far achieved in dressage. Of course, not all my memories of this time are happy ones. There were days when I trained to the limits of endurance and was almost in tears because I thought I would never be able to achieve what was expected of me. Nor did Don make it any easier for me.

A horse with a mind of his own, it was very difficult for him to accede to a rider, and time and time again he would try to get the upper hand. However, when he did accept the rider's help, he was marvelous—the only

Inge and Pascal (38) perform a pirouette in canter (26-37).

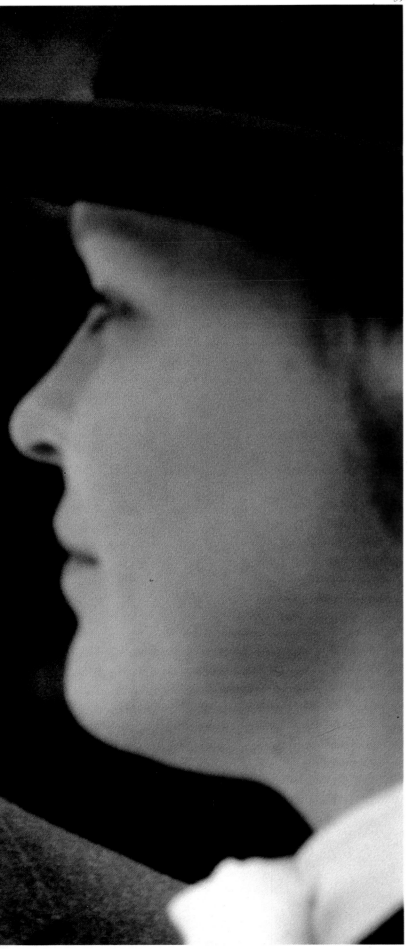

problem was to get him to accept it. What can you do with a horse that refuses to enter the dressage hall or the arena? I can't tell you the tricks my uncle and I were reduced to using to outwit that horse. There were exhibitions where the only way I could get him into the hall was to lead him in backward.

Once, a few years ago, I was taking part with Don Benito in a junior examination in Leverkusen. The place where we were to appear was only about ten minutes from our stables, and the ring itself was bordered by grandstands and trees that blocked off the view of the riding grounds. The problems started during the untying. Don knew the way back to his stall perfectly well and, paying no attention to me at all, kept trying to get back there. Only by the greatest efforts could I keep him on the starting square. He had already run back to the stables twice. My starting time was drawing closer and I still hadn't been able to get him into the dressage square. He was much more interested in a chestnut tree beside the grandstand. Only after several minutes' struggle was I able to ride smartly

Before a competition Fritz Templemann gives Inge last-minute instructions (39). Mrs. Templemann checks Inge's hair and her jacket (40), which is decorated with important German awards (41).

into the square. But success was short-lived. After the salutation, Don stood as if rooted in the first corner, ignoring my frantic efforts to get him to move. The disqualification bell rang; the first note was still hanging in the air when Don raised his ears, immediately turned round, and left the square at a very expressive trot.

Don's acting up has decreased over the past four years, owing to my perseverance and my uncle's patience. We could certainly never have established by force the sort of confidence that exists between us now. It is to this confidence that I owe one of my most beautiful memories of dealing with horses. During my free periods at school, I often used to make a side trip to the stables. This day, long before I reached the riding hall, I could tell by the uproar

Inge and Paquito prepare to enter the competition square (42) where the judges are waiting (43). Once on the square (44) Inge knows that each of her movements will be carefully followed by the judges.

that something was up. I went into the hall and, sure enough, it was Don Benito. He had managed to get loose, and several riders and a lot of people on foot were trying to round him up and get him back into his stall. Don quite obviously was not planning to relinquish his new-found freedom so soon. While Don continued his game, I laid bets with his pursuers that I could get him to follow me. Despite feeling a little insecure because of the general skepticism, I went to the middle of the hall and called him. He pricked up his ears, immediately galloped over to me and remained standing quietly in front of me, as if to say, "You finally got here." This success meant more to me than all my winnings.

Don Benito and I continued to develop together under my uncle's expert training, so that in the past few years we made the jump from the L, M and S dressages and the FEI examination all the way to the Grand Prix. So far, the greatest success of our career together was our double victory in the Junior European Masters Competition in 1977 and 1978, in the individual as well as the team competitions. For myself the first European Masters Competition was the greatest victory, since I, as an individual entrant (actually an outsider), carried the German flag. I was only taken into the team as a replacement because we had lost our most favored rider. No one imagined the team would have the least chance of success with Don and me. And no doubt this was the deciding factor—when there is nothing to lose, you can only win and are therefore willing to take any risk. I think that more than anything else, this sense of fatalism carried me to victory in three of the necessary riding tests. Also, the competition was held at Leverkusen on the very square Don had made such a fuss about entering the year before.

The outlook for the second European Masters was worse, from a psychological point of view. As the defender of the title, one is naturally the favorite, which arouses expectations in everyone, not the least in oneself. Therefore, the victory is, in the final analysis, more the vindication of one's hopes than an exceptional achievement. In such a situation it is immediately clear how important strong nerves are. Any nervousness is instantly transmitted to the horse and leads to errors that would normally not be made. Luckily, I do not suffer from nerves, and this gives me a certain advantage over other riders. In any case, I retained the title.

Meanwhile, I am riding in the Senior Class and the Grand Prix and the Grand Prix Special. These are the most difficult of all the dressage examinations and require Olympic standards. The highest demands are made of both horse and rider and their fulfillment demands added

(45-47) Inge cues her horse for the half pass; front legs crossed, back legs crossed, front legs crossed. In (48) she is seen in the extended trot.

concentration, ability and practice, all of which, I must say, add greatly to the pleasure. Each time, horse and rider must exert a total effort to complete one of these tests successfully, and in the many compulsory exercises there will always be weak points to be overcome.

At the end of this year's season, I can only say that Don and I both need a lot more training and practice before we can achieve a truly good Grand Prix. Naturally Don is not the only horse I ride. Every day except for one day's rest a week I ride from two to four horses. How much time I can spend at the stables depends on how much time I can spare from my studies at the university, for even though I would like to give preference to riding, a profession is a major priority. But I hope to be able to combine the two life-styles in the future.

The contestants wait nervously (49) for the decision of the judges. Inge and Paquito with awards (50 & 51).

VICKY SMALLWOOD
usa

F or several seasons I had been photographing horse races for a future book. I panned and shot from every possible angle and at every possible shutter speed, but no matter what I tried, there was nothing unique about my photographs. Finally, I came upon a place in Europe where horses are still raced on the beach, right at the tide line, and it was only then that I was able to come up with the pictures I wanted.

The time I had spent on the first unusable photographs, though, was by no means wasted. The excitement of those mornings and afternoons on the track was worth every minute—I love horse racing.

So I looked forward to the section of this book that would take me to a track where I wouldn't have to worry about coming up with unique racing photos, but simply document several days in the life of a girl jockey. For this chapter I enlisted the aid of my friend, trainer Jim Fresques, who has a jockey school in southern California. It was Jim's wife, Rita, who found Vicky Smallwood riding at Rillito Downs in Tucson, Arizona.

Jim flew with me from Los Angeles to Tucson, where the following afternoon I met and started to photograph Vicky. For the first race there, fortunately, I had a camera at the end of the stretch and captured the accident shown in the following pages. Horse racing is a dangerous, tough business, and Vicky Smallwood, against great odds in this man's world, has had no easy time. At times she seemed anxious to cooperate, at others she made a difficult subject. In spite of this, I liked her, and it became a challenge literally to stalk and photograph her at the track.

I was born eighteen years ago in Fort Worth, Texas. When I was eight, my father, a sergeant in the U.S. Marine Corps, was transferred to Cherry Point, North Carolina, where we lived until his retirement. The family then moved to a farm in New Boston, Texas, and it was there that I owned my first horse.

(1) Texas-born jockey Vicky Smallwood with a Thoroughbred that she has just exercised.

I had my first experience with horses when I was six years old. My grandmother owned three ponies: two white fillies and a brown stallion. Young as I was, I would ride around the yard on the bigger filly with only a halter and a lead rope. Those rides ended the day the stallion chased us through a barbed wire fence.

While at Cherry Point, I hung around a riding stable where I learned how to ride jumping horses. When I was fourteen years old and we returned to Texas, I changed my riding habit for boots and Levis. When I finally got my own horse, I taught him to run around barrels instead of leaping over fences. From bareback to a flat saddle, to a stock saddle, and finally to a jockey's saddle, my life has revolved around horses.

Having drifted in and out of trouble, I wasn't much help to my folks. So when I finished my junior year of high school, I decided to strike out on my own. First I went to live with a girl friend, and for two weeks I looked for a job. But there are not many jobs open for a sixteen-year-old girl with little education. Then, by some darn stroke of luck, I got a phone call from a jockey who dated my best girl friend. He was looking for riders to work for him on a training farm in De Kalb, Texas. I took the job and worked for a month, learning to gallop the two- and three-year-old colts in training, before deciding to follow the circuit and gallop horses on the track.

Vicky picks up extra money galloping horses at dawn at Rillito Downs in Arizona (2 & 4). Waiting for another mount, she pauses at the hot walker (3).

For a year and a half I followed the circuit, working as an exercise girl. The early morning hours of each weekday were filled with all the hustle and bustle of track life. On a good morning I'd gallop eight head of horses, making five dollars a ride. Saturday and Sunday afternoons I spent hanging over the rail watching my friends race, studying them.

Boy, how I waited for my first break to ride. It almost came at a Quarter-horse track in New York called Parr Meadows. A trainer with whom I'd been working asked me if I'd ride for him. Still rather unsure of myself, I asked him for two weeks to get in some extra practice, especially in breaking from the gate. Then I could apply for my jockey license and ride for him. Bad luck. The track went broke and closed down within those two weeks.

Vicky puts on her helmet (5) and later waits to mount (6). She receives instructions from a trainer (7). After crossing the paddock (8), she passes through a tunnel and onto the track (9).

My chance came later in Commonwealth, Kentucky, with a trainer called Howard Radiger. I didn't win, but even though I was scared and my stomach was full of butterflies, I stayed with my horse and rode a pretty good race. From River Downs in Ohio to Delta and Evangeline Downs in Louisiana, I rode ninety-two horses before I won my first race. Then I won three races at Evangeline, a track where only two other girls rode.

I came to Arizona in September 1979, and went straight to Globe and rode a few horses. My best day in Globe was when I picked up a mount in the Gila County Derby that was a 25-1 longshot and won the race by three lengths. When that track closed I came on to the Rillito track in Tucson. From November to February 1980, I won ten races there.

Once the horses are in the gate, Vicky tenses with the other jockeys (10). As the horses break from the gate, Vicky shouts to her mount (11). In white silks she is caught up in the bunch (12).

(13) Pounding toward the finish line, the second horse from the right starts to break down, having broken its shoulder. Two horses were killed in this accident. Vicky's red-and-white cap with the initials VS can be seen fourth from the left (16).

17

18

19

20

21

22

(18) It looks as if the riders on the left will gallop around the fallen horse. However, in (20) it is clear that the jockey directly in front of

Vicky is about to crash. In (21) Vicky can be seen starting to turn her mount just in time (22 & 23) to avoid the fallen horses.

23

My day starts at seven in the morning and ends about three hours later. I show up at the barns and wait for my first horse. The horses are brought in fully tacked; I only need to bring my hard hat and crop. The trainer legs me up on the small exercise saddle and gives me instructions for his horse. I turn the horse toward the track for his morning workout. In ten minutes I'll be back. Then I turn the sweating horse over to his trainer and wait for the next one.

After my morning work, I'll visit with friends in the kitchen. The talk is about the only thing we have time to

Vicky's expression (25) needs no comment. On the photo of the finish, Vicky indicates the blur of the fallen horse just behind which she can be seen on number five (26).

know—horse racing. Around eleven I'll head back to my apartment and sit in front of the television watching the "soaps." On weekday evenings my friends and I go discoing. On the weekends I go to sleep early before race day.

I've been lucky so far not to have had spills. I figure someday it'll happen to me, but I don't like to think about it. Since I don't belong to the Jockey Guild, I'm not covered by an insurance policy. So if I get injured, the race track and I would have to pay for my hospitalization. As long as luck stays with me, it's a waste of time and money to belong to the Guild. After all, they don't get me my work. Why should they have a piece of my check?

If I've had one big disappointment in my life as a jockey, it's that I've never been able to have one close friend. Following the circuit I don't have time for a close friend outside the racing world, and when a track

Up in the saddle Vicky (in white) gets a good start out of the gate (27). Toward the middle of the pack, Vicky (in black) fights for position on a muddy track (28 & 29).

28

31

32

33

34

35

36

37

closes, I may or may not go to the same track that my friends do. But I've become very close to my family since leaving home. I call or write to them at least once a week and always try to make it home for the holidays. My folks were upset when I left home to ride horses, but they knew they couldn't hold me. After seeing how dedicated I've been during the last few years, they have nothing but support for me.

The racing world is full of difficulties for us young jockeys. When you're just new to the game, you have mostly second-rate horses to ride, making it difficult to chalk up any wins. Only with your wins can you get some better horses. Apart from galloping fees, the majority of

Galloping down the straight for home, Vicky (in white) fights to take the lead (30-38).

38

jockeys earn about a $25 mount fee for each race (depending on the track) and 10 percent of the purse if you win.

When a track closes, the jockeys usually follow a trainer who has asked them, or for whom they enjoy riding, to the next track. I hope someday a top trainer will like the way I ride and ask me to ride at one of the big tracks for him. Only on the big-money horses can a jockey make his fortune. I'm not all that sure of my future, though. Those lucky breaks are hard to come by, and even harder when you're a girl. Most of the oldtimers around the tracks are still not convinced that a woman can ride as well as a man. I feel she can, but it'll still take a few more years to convince the men.

I've never had a weight problem. I eat pretty much what I want and always try to eat a large breakfast on the morning before races. My ability to maintain my weight without dieting is a decided advantage over most of the men. I don't have to weaken my system in order to stay under the maximum weight allowance.

Twenty years from now I hope still to be riding. If not, I suppose I'll be a housewife, though I don't plan on getting married until I'm at least twenty-five years old. My major goal right now is to earn enough money to buy myself a new pickup truck and a fifth-wheel trailer; so I'll keep riding, hoping to get a break here and there on a good horse, in a good race, at a good track.

A winner's smile (40 & 41). In (42) Vicky points to herself winning on number five. Waiting for her next race, she studies the program and jokes with other jockeys (43).

43

CLAUDIA
FEH
france

O ne day in 1979 I was photographing horses at the biological research station of Tour du Valat in the Camargue when I discovered I was being observed through binoculars by a young woman. I waved to her, but she ignored me and went on her way toward the herd I had been taking pictures of, pausing from time to time only to dictate into a tape recorder.

That was my first introduction to Claudia Feh, a retiring young Swiss biologist, who for the past six years has been conducting a study of the ecology and social behavior of a free-living herd of Camargue horses. When we were introduced more formally later that evening, I asked her what she had been doing. "Watching you," she said. "I'm very protective of the horses and like to make sure that they aren't being bothered."

I spent six days at Tour du Valat taking pictures and discussing horses by the hour with Claudia. We became great friends, and this shy young woman, whose greatest concern is that people do not overromanticize and anthropomorphize the half-wild creatures she loves so much and has studied so long under the harshest of conditions, was who I thought of first when I finally decided to begin work on this book.

I don't think there were any horses in the middle of Zurich where I was born. Nor did I see many during my childhood, spent in the same town. But, like everybody, I wanted to have a pony on the balcony. I thought a pony would be much better than a horse as it was smaller. My parents told me the pony would be unhappy, so I started to breed frogs, with great success because soon there were thirty-two frogs jumping all around; eventually they took possession of the whole apartment. My mother had difficulty explaining to others living in the building where they came from, so I had to take them back to the pond.

(1) Equine behaviorist Claudia Feh with her own Camargue horse.

When I was five my parents left my brother and me for the first time and went on holiday in Provence and the Camargue. They brought back a toy black bull for my brother and a small china horse for me.

The only way to get close to horses in Switzerland was to ride them. At ten I had saved enough money to start taking riding lessons. The money was soon gone, but meanwhile I had found a cheaper way to ride: I exercized horses for other people. Most of these horses were young and difficult to ride.

I first went to the Camargue when I was sixteen and had not completely recovered from a broken head. One of the young, difficult horses had thrown me against a wall, not just once but three times, which was definitely too many times. Maybe that is the reason I could never get the Camargue out of my head. That and the fact that it was the first time I had seen a group of horses playing together in an immense field. They seemed to laugh, and I just stared at them and laughed too. I think that was the moment I decided to live there one day.

(2) Claudia walks the lane from the horse pasture to the research station. (3) Claudia with (left to right) Dr. Luc Hoffmann, founder and director of the research station, Bettina Hughes, one of the originators of the program, and Dr. Patrick Duncan, director of the horse study program at Tour du Valat. Sometimes Claudia uses a bicycle to get from the research station to the horse pasture (4).

After making that decision, I had three years to dream about it and wait, before finishing high school, which made everything terrible. After school was finished there was nothing left to do but to go and live in the Camargue after all those dreams.

Through a friend of a friend, I heard about a biological station there, so I wrote them a letter. The station at that time was mainly an ornithological ringing center. They needed assistants to control the nests and to do bird counts. I had no qualifications whatsoever for such work,

but Bettina Hughes, the girl in charge of employment, thought I would be all right. Two months later I arrived in the Camargue thinking I was the happiest human being alive. I have never changed my mind about that.

It was the first time I had met really passionate people, passionate about their lives. Work was a part of it, the main part to be sure. Dr. Luc Hoffmann could talk for hours about world wildlife conservation, Heinz about his egrets, Alan about flamingoes, John about his bird expeditions and Herbert about any bird. There was one aim:

nature conservation. There was one philosophy: everybody had the right to live his own life as he thought best.

I did not forget the horses among all the birds. Horses were everywhere, living outside day and night, occasionally used for work with the bulls or at the station to

(5) The horse range is a semi-wild area also inhabited by many kinds of birds such as the cattle egret shown here. If a horse approaches (6), the observer remains still to be sniffed at (7), after which the horse walks away (8).

count birds. Every Wednesday I went on horseback to the reserve, which covers 32,000 acres. That meant nine hours without seeing another human being or a house; nothing but birds, water, the salt flats and the ears of my horse.

After a year Dr. Hoffmann and Bettina wanted me to get serious again, which meant going back to Zurich and the university. So the dreaming started again. The dreams were, nevertheless, much more precise now. I had left my own horse, a small house someone had lent me, and the country I loved.

I spent about five months of my first year at the university pretending to work for my chemistry examinations, but I was, in fact, in the Camargue. What I was doing primarily was working for the World Wildlife Fund of Switzerland and chopping firewood to get some kind of human temperature into the five rooms of my house during the winter. I had a motorbike to go to the next village, which was about five kilometers away; the next closest was about thirty kilometers' distance. However, the bike never wanted to go on humid days, so I stayed home or rode my

Carrying a tape recorder (9), Claudia spends hours with the herd, waiting to observe behavior such as mutual grooming (10 & 11).

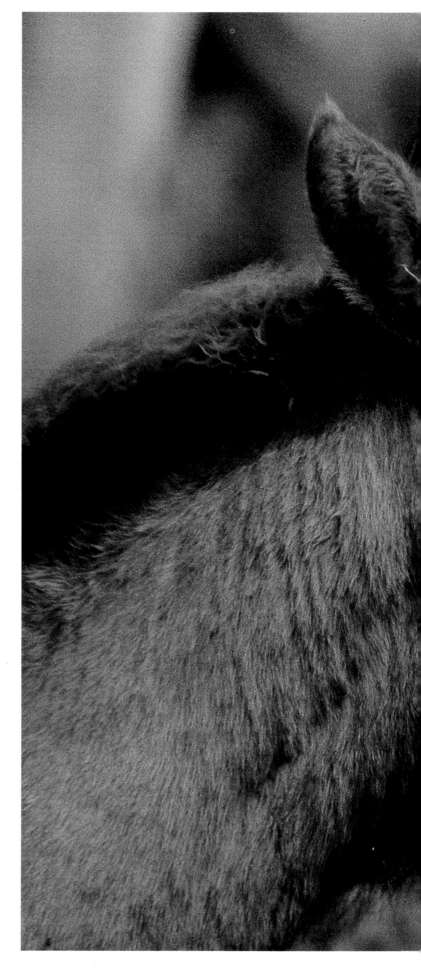

horse, which at this stage I was training to become a "siesta horse." I thought it would be nice to be able to lie on a horse for an hour and look at the clouds or the stars; of course, without saddle, bridle or anything. I succeeded in doing it several years later.

(12) Two stallions tensely smell one another. When the horse on the left rears up (13), the horse on the right displays threat, flexing his muzzle and rolling his eyes. Here it is the horse on the right who threatens to attack (14). Both horses rear up at one another (15).

15

During this year the plans I had already made were reinforced; I wanted to work and live with, and for, free-living animals. I especially wanted to try and understand their lives. Then one night Bettina's letter arrived: "We have just released thirteen horses in an eight-hundred-acre pasture at Tour du Valat, to start a five-year project on the ecology and social behavior of a free-living herd in the Camargue. We will test observation methods and start this spring. Would you like to be a field assistant?"

The first day back in the Camargue I went out to see the horses. I stopped at a distance and watched them through binoculars. I wanted to be sure they were free horses and that nobody had the right to touch them or make them do anything for five years.

Horse behavior Claudia is on the watch for: (17) self-grooming using the teeth; (18) yawning; (19) teeth clapping, a subordinate gesture used by a threatened foal; (20) self-grooming using a hoof tip; (21) stallion-harem relationships (the lead stallion is the white horse nearest Claudia); feeding (22); and selfgrooming using grass, dust or mud (23).

21

Then we started: two teams of two people, armed with tape recorders, stopwatches and binoculars, working in four-hour periods from seven in the morning until seven at night. Every five minutes one observer noted the basic activity of each horse, if it was grazing, standing, resting, lying down, walking, and so on. Every half an hour the same observer drew a position map of all the animals to determine later which horse was nearest which. Every hour he marked the exact position of the herd on a map that showed the vegetation in the pasture. The second observer, during this time, followed each horse for fifteen minutes and dictated into the tape recorder all its interactions with the other horses.

(24-40) Claudia studies a play fight that starts with muzzle sniffing (24), followed by lunging and biting (26 & 27). A kick threat (28) is given, after which the young stallions engage in mane pulling and rearing (29-32).

The first observation period lasted four months, from March until June, then again in November. The second year the ecological study was intensified. Patrick, the ecologist, decided to watch the horses at night, and so we started a forty-eight-hour program; twice a month for one year, a team of five people watched the horses continuously for two days and nights, to establish their use of time during different seasons. In four-hour blocks we again noted activities every five minutes for each horse, with the help of a light intensifier. A second observer stayed in the laboratory listening to the walkie-talkie, waiting for "help" calls when the herd separated into subgroups or became too dispersed.

When the light gray stumbles (35), his opponent grasps him by the neck (36 & 37). The dark horse continues to keep a firm grip on the light one's neck (38, 39 & 40). These play fights can last for as long as half an hour.

We seldom had to give up, but I remember one night Sue, Patrick and I found ourselves by chance on the track, white from frost, and not a sound of a horse was to be heard in the foggy night. We had to start again the following day.

Changes in the herd occurred during those first two years. Six foals had been born during the first spring, seven the second. Darius, the dominant stallion, was still the only adult stallion, but G-4, the three-year-old son of the old dominant mare, 9, started to become interested in other mares. He had left the side of his mother and attached himself to one of Darius's mares and followed her around the whole day. He covered all of Darius's other females as well. The situation did not last. After some fights with Darius (neither got wounded), G-4 had to leave the herd. He went to join the other young stallions, which had lived alone in the southern part of the pasture since the beginning of the study. It was the start of the stallion group.

At the beginning of the project's third year, I started my own study on the development of the social behavior of stallions. Professor Tschanz from Berne, who had initiated the original study with Bettina, agreed to supervise my work scientifically, and Patrick promised to help. I became a student at the University of Marseilles to do an "outside-university" thesis.

Serious fights between older animals generally last only seconds. The two stallions Claudia is watching threaten each other (42, 43 & 44) before rearing up (45). In most fights it seems there is a mutual agreement that neither horse will bite or kick too hard. This silent truce is illustrated here (46-50) before both stallions drop back to the ground (52).

That May I started a pilot study to test the methods I had chosen. After two weeks of observation, the stallions suddenly started to cooperate—too well. Darius chased five of the young males out of the herd in three weeks, and they all joined the stallion group in the south. I didn't know where to look, there was so much interaction going on. I spent up to fifteen hours a day in the field. However, everything calmed down again, and the tedious work of longtime observation started; five days a week, three weeks a month, month after month, for two and a half years. When I came in from the field, I had to transcribe my tapes onto specially prepared sheets and analyze the data. The first winter was very calm; the four yearling stallions I watched stayed with their mothers, sisters or brothers, occasionally playing with each other.

Spring returned, and with it, activity. The oldest stallions of the stallion group went to visit the herd. During the first few days, they just stayed at a distance and looked at Darius's mares. Then they attacked. G-4 tried to abduct two mares, and H-4 tried to attach himself to one of the old mares. Darius had to fight three stallions at the same time. Forty-eight hours later, after more or less continuous encounters and rounding up of his herd, he had to

A gray foal teasing a brown one attracts Claudia's attention (54). After having had his mane pulled, the brown foal flees with the gray in pursuit (55), almost knocking into Claudia as they pass her (56 & 57).

give up. He was unrecognizable. Bleeding from a wound at the nostrils, head down and completely covered with mud, he seemed hardly able to move a leg. G-4 went off with his mare, and H-4 remained in the middle of the herd.

Then it was quiet again, and we had to wait until the next spring to see other big events. Gradually, over the next few years, Darius lost mares to the other young stallions and finally ended up with only the two dominant ones.

The situation now resembles that of other free-living horses and zebras: There are several bands, each composed of one or two adult stallions and one to four mares with their offspring, which generally stay with the band for two or three years. Young mares are usually absorbed into a band when they have had their first foal.

The strongest bond in horses is between mother and foal, followed by the attachment of a foal to his siblings, stallions to mares and young horses to other young horses. Now, six years since the beginning of the study, there are eighty-nine horses. The herd stays together most of the time and only during resting periods are the different bands clearly visible. The nine adult stallions know each other's strengths and positions very well. They fight from time to time but much more often they perform their stallion-ritual. While fighting, they seem to avoid hurting each other. Not one of them has had a serious wound up until now. Why should they? They can have everything they need without hurting one another.

In five years the horses have developed from a more or less domestic system to a wild one. I have had to stop field work and am now writing my thesis. I still go to see them regularly, and sometimes I dream about a really wild herd, in a pasture without a fence.

On the porch of her house, Claudia takes notes from her tape-recorded observations (58). Claudia is riding her own horse through the marsh (59), followed by her donkey and a Camargue colt.

EPILOGUE

T *raveling from country to country, I met many girls whose careers were with horses. None, however, touched me as deeply as Andrea Bolton, a quiet young woman who is an extremely good wildlife painter from Portland, Oregon. I met Andy while I was photographing Debi Jenson at Raintree Egyptian Stud.*

Often Andy would visit the ranch and quietly watch what we were doing with the horses; other times she would photograph us at work. Apart from saying hello now and then, I had little conversation with her and would not be thinking about her now if, on my last night at Raintree, she hadn't driven out to give me this letter:

I do not presume to suggest to you how you might write and compose your art and books; I am certain there are many persons who have suggested good, bad and otherwise. I only present this to you for your consideration. Please do not forget the girls who love horses with all their souls but who have never owned one.

For the most part, I believe that nearly every girl who has seen a horse, or been near a horse, dreams of owning one; but as girls grow up the dreams become only a wish

that fades and often dies when they reach the age that boys become important to them. There are even girls who have a horse or a pony that will eventually stand idle, no longer loved or needed, then sold when one boyfriend, then another, comes along.

But there are still those who love horses with all that is in them—but have never owned one. Some of the reasons are lack of finance or even, at times, lack of family interest or understanding, plus lack of the necessary space. These girls follow their horse-owning friends to 4-H meetings, shows and even to the barn when they go out to ride. You sit on the fence and watch the horse disappear into the trees and you sit waiting, wishing, hoping and dreaming. When the offer of a ride is made, it is gratefully and enthusiastically accepted. Even if it might be only once around an arena—the moment is cherished.

As you grow older the hunger and longing grow with you—but as the responsibility that comes with age and maturity increases, you are forced to suppress the need—but not the love. There may be a brief opportunity when a horse might be at hand. You scheme and pull together resources in blind hope—only to wake up to practicality and a realization that the money needed for the

purchase is not enough—though all you have. You let go. You cry.

Love stays—and it never diminishes, though you allow it to hide. Hope is the small light that keeps you going. If you should find this girl somewhere in your travels—please consider her with the others.

*I*t was this letter that made me realize that the Debi Jensens, the Inge Schultzes and the Mercedes Gonzálezes represent only a fortunate handful of all those girls in love with horses. There are thousands and thousands of girls like Andrea Bolton who care for horses just as passionately, but who will never own one. Perhaps the young women in this book will inspire others to push hard enough to acquire a horse of their own one day. For those who, like Andrea, may never have that opportunity, I hope that sharing in the lives of the eleven girls pictured here will provide a joyful and exciting experience. This book would be incomplete if its last chapter was not dedicated to Andrea and others like her who form the majority of all those girls in love with horses.

ACKNOWLEDGEMENTS

My deepest thanks go to the following people who contributed generously to the accomplishment of this book: Canada (Calgary) — Ron Cole, Don Fleming, and Gary Coleman; USA (San Juan Bautista, Calif.) Elizabeth Searle, Jeff Moore, Joyce Post, and Inez Fort, (Hollywood, Calif.) the producers of Little House on the Prairie, *and of* Charlie Chan and the Curse of the Dragon Lady, *and Carl Pitti, Jeff Ramsey, Kurt Vavra, Dick Broün, and Darlene La Madrid, (Oregon) Betty and Bill Notley, (Arizona) Jim Fresques, Heather Ramsey, Jim Wilson, and Bob Allison, (Boise, Idaho) Jack and Alice Blake, Shannon Fleming and Alice Southerland; England — Marilyn Tennent; Mexico — Anita Sentovic, Jorge D. Soler, Rosalinda Soler Gutiérrez, María Antinea Soler Solís, Antonio Solís, Guadalupe Soler de Juárez and the members of the Escaramuza Charra of Tijuana; Germany — Rudolf Blanckenstein, Mr & Mrs Fritz Templemann, Bernard Schulze, Wendy Snowdon and Ole Hoyer; France — Dr Luc Hoffmann and Patrick Duncan; Spain — Alfonso González, Alvaro Domecq Romero, Luis Ramos Paúl, Paco Muñoz, Edla Teele and the riders of the Andalusian School of Equestrian Art.*

For the editing of this manuscript Matthew Robinson has my appreciation as does Diane Haun and Perdita Hordern for typing it. For continued encouragment I thank Larry Hughes, Al Marchioni, Howard Cady and Gloria Loomis. Elías García and the staff of Cromoarte did the finest possible job making the color separations, and José Pedro Hernández and Florida Fotocomposición again proved to be good friends in setting the English text. For continued enthusiasm from start to finish of this project, I thank my assistant, José Franco Cadena.

The film used for most of the photographs was Ektachrome 200. Cameras used were two Nikon Fs equipped with motor drives, a 50-300 Nikkor zoom lens and a 28 mm wide angle lens.